Jude's Letter for Today's Path

Help for the Struggling and Dealing With Ungodliness

R F Pennington

Copyright 2010 by the author of this book, R F Pennington.
The book author retains sole copyright
to his contributions to this book.

Published 2010.
Second Edition. Published 2013.
Printed in the United States of America by Lightning Source Inc.

Cover photo by Dee Pennington.

All Scripture quotations are from the New American Standard Bible
© 1975, Lockman Foundation. All Greek Dictionary citings © 1981,
Lockman Foundation. Reproduction permission granted through
Foundation Press Publications, publisher for the
Lockman Foundation.

This book published by BookCrafters,
Joe and Jan McDaniel.
SAN 859-6352
bookcrafters@comcast.net

ISBN 978-1-937862-25-1
Library of Congress Control Number 201291936

Copies of this book may be ordered at
www.bookcrafters.net
and other online bookstores.

Dedication

A big *Thanks!* to Charles Speer for making me write this in the first place. I hope when I sat at your feet those years ago that I wasn't too much trouble. Another *Thanks!* to all of my instructors at Sunset International Bible Institute, some of which have passed, that instilled in me the importance of I Timothy 4:16 above all else as a Minister.

Foreword

The original assignment was passed out in a Biblical Interpretations class by my instructor, Charles Speer, while my wife, Dee, and I were attending the Sunset International Bible Institute. The assignment was short, but nowhere near simple- -*write a commentary on the letter from Jude*. By this point in the game, I knew better than to put off this assignment for very long. Surrounding myself with prayer cover (best thing), with several translations of the New Testament (next best thing), Greek dictionaries (essential!) and dozens of commentaries (OK, I guess) I dove into oblivion for what seemed like hours every day for about eight or ten weeks and turned up, on one ancient Macintosh computer, a thirty-page-large-headers-and-footers-space-and-a-half-large-font tome. Feeling pretty proud of this accomplishment, I asked someone to proof it for me. Upon examining the not-so-large by book standards work, that someone remarked, "Kinda small for a book isn't it?" To which I replied, "But the Book of Jude is only less than a page long!" Undaunted, I turned it in. I don't remember what my grade was.

I really don't.

So why would we need to spend time dissecting something as seemingly self-evident and ever so short as the Book of Jude? Why resurrect an old class assignment and rehash it on a state of the art computer (still Mac, of course)? Answer, because the stakes are too high, those stakes being our eternal destiny and the outcome of the local church.

Throughout this work you will find abbreviations for the books of the Bible. They are the standard two to five letter abbreviations and shouldn't pose too great a threat. Also, don't let the Greek words drive you off. Sometimes we need to look at the original Greek word that the New Testament writer used and do a little word study on it. Consider it like going to the dentist: quick and painless!

Also, as in all my writings, I will use words and titles that not all are used to. I use pastor, preacher, minister, priest, shepherd, deacon, elder, presbyter, sanctuary, auditorium, annex, Bible class, Sunday school, disciple, saint and I'm running out of words here. I use these terms because these terms are used today. Some you may not use. I intend to run no one off, rather, I intend to reach out to all people everywhere from every flavor so that we may reach for what really matters in our spiritual walk: walking with, and like, Christ.

Table of Contents

Why We Need Jude Today 1

General Introduction to Jude 6

The Author and Authenticity of Jude 9

Recipients of Jude 12

Occasion and Purpose of Jude 14

Date and Place of Writing of Jude 18

Unique Features of Jude 19

The Outline 22

The Commentary 24

Introduction to Jude, vs 1-4 26

Ungodliness Will Receive the Judgment of God, verses 5-16 34

Christians Will Escape the Wrath of God, verses 17-25 56

Why We Need Jude Today

It is almost routine now that churches fold and close their doors. Not just in little drying up farming communities, but large churches that had hundreds in attendance. Why? Were they disbanding in order to go together with other churches and create a megachurch? Some did, but the total numbers of Christians keeps dropping. Would Jude's warnings have helped keep the doors open?

If the church isn't folding, it is sometimes going the other way---doctrines so strange that one returns home after visiting the church's worship, opens the Yellow Pages, and makes sure that this place was listed under the heading CHURCH. Would Jude's warnings have helped keep that church on a doctrinal path to Heaven? That, you will decide after reading this book and the book of Jude. But Jude's letter isn't just about churches in general.

On an individual scale, we need help as disciples of Christ. Many years ago my wife, Dee, and I attended a spiritual workshop in Illinois. Three days of intense lectures, where keynote speakers hashed out the issues of the day, parsed Greek and Hebrew words, and exegeted the Scriptures to capture the finer points of what the scholars would have us know. During a break, as folks were running here and there to catch the next speaker, a man was asked if he was enjoying the lecture. He replied, "I'm not sure what everyone is talking about here. I'm a new Christian and I'm just trying to find help to quit smoking and find thirty minutes a day to read my Bible."

A lamb stood in a den of Daniels. We were straining out gnats in the lecture halls and leaving one to choke on the weightier matters of the Law.

Just as a child needs help in learning to tie his shoes, so we need the same basic level of help when we first come to

Christ as newborn babies, freshly uprooted out of the most vile and hideous kingdom ever imaginable. Some will grow and some will not. Soon, or maybe not so soon, we learn to tie our shoelaces, however, we never stop being children in God's kingdom here on earth.

The Scriptures speak of the children of God and makes no mention that we ever grow into adulthood per sé. While on earth, we remain in this wonderful family that we call the church--all the time dealing with each other, watching some refuse to learn to tie their shoes, encouraging those who have learned to, crying with those who tried too early and are now experiencing failure, warning others that know better about tying their shoes and crying for those who did not listen and have now tripped and fallen across their own shoelaces, of their own doing.

For all of the problems of the church, it is still a pretty good place to spend our pre-eternity. We will always fuss and choose sides among ourselves. We will always pick at each other, pick at the preacher, the pastor, the deacons, the layout of our services and the color of the carpet in the foyer! Let's face it--we are human beings with wants, wishes, motivations and desires. Though we are never excused from maintaining peace and harmony, for the most part we know deep down inside that we all have a common ground, a common love and a common Father in Heaven. But not everyone who 'goes to church' has the same agenda as we do.

One stands outside our family. He has been described as a roaring lion here and the father of lies there. To look at him, however, we would only see beauty, an angel of light. He accuses, tricks, lies and we have no record that he is ever on vacation or taking a nap. To make matters more serious, he has a host of those at his disposal, ready to do his bidding--and we can't even see them! The attacks on our Christianity come at the rate of constant. The attacks from without are easier to distinguish, however. For example, legal decisions against the family of God and the hindrance of our shoe tying are easy to spot. We know that this kind of attack cannot come from above--but can only come from below. We will drop our petty bickering at a moment's notice and ready ourselves on the wall for this kind of frontal attack. However, Trojan

Horses are much harder to see through. Termites do their work behind the walls.

For example, have you ever heard, or pondered, anything such as:

- I remember the night when brother Fred gave his commitment to Jesus and that was twenty one years ago. Surely he isn't mixed up in all of this?!
- Well, the elders and the pastor certainly wouldn't lead us in the wrong direction, would they?!
- We've pretty much been doing this for the last ever-so-long as I can remember, so surely we must be right on in the Scriptures, aren't we?!
- The sermons seem different these days. I'm guessing that the minister is just having a bad run at it. He's been under a lot of stress. I don't really believe that he really believes some of the things that he has been saying, does he?!
- Brother Ferbie has been a pastor around here for most of my life. I guess he's pretty much on target, isn't he?!
- Sister Mabel has been teaching the twelve year old girls since I was a twelve year old girl. God must be with her since she's been a teacher this long, isn't He?!
- I really don't understand that announcement that was made yesterday in worship. It almost sounded like we were going to start doing something that the Bible knows nothing about. Surely our shepherds wouldn't lead us into something like that, would they?!

Perhaps. Perhaps not. But the one thing for certain is that the longer Satan has his grips around the hearts and minds of the influential--the feeders of the flock--the more widespread the devastation is, if and when the cover is lifted and the covey flushed. Depending on where you worship, what flavor of disciple you are, what creed you subscribe to, your feeders will go by different names: Pastors, Ministers, Cell Leaders, Priests, Deacons, Elders, Preachers, Shepherds, Home Leaders, Presbyters, and the list is longer. This is not an attempt to wade through the differing names. This is an attempt to bring Jude alive to both you and your local church where you meet. It is an attempt to keep Satan from both you and your spiritual family.

For our time and place, we need not worry about demon possession. Why? Quite simply, that would be Bad PR on Satan's part. Why advertise yourself? No, in our time and place in the sun Satan has us, by and large, through material possession. Alongside material possession comes a host of egos, evil desires and false foundations. Jesus predicted this in the parable of the soils when he said:

The worries of the world, and the deceitfulness of riches, and the desires for other things enter in and choke the word, and it becomes unfruitful. Mk 4

Any one of these things by themselves will choke out the word. Place a combination of these things together with overblown egos set upon a rocky course and the devastation is not only full blown, but it comes quicker than the afternoon express. Not one stone will remain standing upon another.

Peter, in both of his letters, shows us hope in the midst of suffering. John reminds us in his letters, in case we missed it in his Gospel, that the standard is Christ. Romans explains to us that we are justified by faith and Galatians warns us of mixing gospel with anything else. Jesus spoke a little something about wolves in sheep's clothing and our need to identify and avoid such in His Sermon on the Mount. The little letter of Jude warns us of the ever possible complete and devastating destruction of the body of Christ through slow decay of falsehood from within, especially from the top down when it comes to local leadership, made up of humans, in the church.

Begin with the two most important steps of Bible study: Pray for wisdom and pause and read the Letter of Jude. One will gain more--on any Bible reading or Bible study--if the habit of reading out of several translations is made. You may have your favorite. I certainly have mine. However, for the sake of study with a fuller understanding, I regularly read out of the New American Standard, American Standard, New International Version, King James Version, The Message... You get the picture.

Let me restate: Pause to pray, then read the letter of Jude. That is where the truth is. This is only a thought, a guide. Continue only after reading Jude.

General Introduction to Jude

Brevity is the most noticeable item when one is introduced to this letter. In other words, super-short. In the sixties, the teenage boys at the Pearl Street Church in Denton, Texas were challenged to read as many Bible books as they could during the Sunday school quarter. Mr. Calvert would pass out stars, stickers or something for each one read. My first book was Jude. What was it about Jude that caught my interest and caused it to be first on the list out of sixty-six Bible entries I could have chosen from? Was it the subject matter? Was it the way that Jude tackled problems head on without apology? Was it because...? No, because it was short and it was already Saturday night. I have since grown a bit in my Bible time.

However, what this letter lacks in length, it makes up in revealing that as the Bible comes to a close, God has not changed His mind on two counts: condemnation of the ungodly and a plea to the spiritual to assist those who struggle with their discipleship. One gets the idea that God is wholly interested in preserving His church. He is. It cost Him Himself on a hill outside of Jerusalem one Friday long ago.

While many an army has hastily retreated, leaving their wounded to the mercy of the advancing enemy, Christianity and the church were never designed to be that kind of army. Isaiah 61:1 and Ezekiel 34:16 show us the master plan from the Master Planner to bind up the wounded:

The Spirit of the Lord God is upon me, because the Lord has anointed me to bring good news to the afflicted; He has sent me to bind up the brokenhearted, to proclaim liberty to captives, and freedom to prisoners; Isaiah

I will seek the lost, bring back the scattered, bind up the broken, and strengthen the sick; but the fat and the strong I will destroy. I will feed them with judgment. Ezekiel

Too often, like a herd of elephants standing around their dead--and then traveling off--we simply do not know what to do with those caught up in the fires of destruction, especially when they are our own. Think back through your Christian life, however short or long that may be, of the seemingly myriad of folks that have wandered away from the fold. How many of those sisters and brothers were the recipients of bad, false or otherwise skewed teachings that they grasped hold of and were pulled out of the fold? How many times were you aware of leaders in the church that had no business being leaders of the church, whether it was from a lack of qualities needed to be a spiritual leader or because their manners, actions and teachings were far less than what the Bible mandated?

Jude only becomes real to us in our time zone when we become real, examining situations in the light of reality.

While this is not an in-depth study of an exhaustive nature (complete with the study of all Greek phrases and words alongside a study of times and backgrounds-aren't you glad?), I believe that this study will be a help to many disciples in gaining a greater appreciation of this one page letter that God, in His providence and will, has given to all mankind for both a warning and for the building up the disciples of Christ. I will leave the academic writing to those more suited. One thing is certain when it comes to Jude: length is inversely proportional to strength. This is one powerful letter. Was then, is now. Have you read it yet?

No, stop and read Jude! "But I did already!" Good, read it again out of another version. Just for grins and giggles I read Jude to myself just now. Took me about 2-1/2 minutes. Just a side note here about Bible reading. While in Bible Boot Camp we were required to read the book of James once a day before class. Well, the semester was ten weeks long and class was every day. You do the math, but twenty years later I can still almost quote James, hit what I'm looking for within a verse or two, but more importantly I know what James says. True for Jude, too. True for you, too, when you read Jude many, many times.

Let's take the time to look at a few items of background such as author, authenticity, occasion, purpose and possible date of writing before we jump into the meat and lessons of Jude. While this may seem academic, it helps place Jude in its context. Anytime a Bible text is taken out of its context it runs the risk of becoming a pretext! While you may read a bit farther and query to yourself, "Is this guy some sort of egghead (I am)?," there is a reason for it. Besides, you paid good money for this book so you might as well read it all. The lessons of Jude will come soon enough. And don't forget to pray.

The Author and Authenticity of Jude

The author of this letter only identifies himself as Jude, the brother of James, and gives no more clue to his identity than what is in verse one. Let's see again what we know for certain about Jude: he was the brother of James. That's it. No more. Well, at least he gives us more than James does in his introduction. Jude, an English form of Judas, was a common name and there have been many candidates as to the author, but only four will be given serious consideration.
1. Judas Barsabbas (Act 15:22)
2. Jude, son of James, an apostle (Lk 6:14*ff*, Act 1:13)
3. Judas of Damascus (Act 9:11)
4. Jude, the brother of the Lord (Mk 6:3)

Judas Barsabbas, the first listed, was a leader in the Jerusalem church and a prophet who was sent with Silas to Antioch of Syria with the apostolic letter. He is not mentioned again in Scripture and nothing is stated about being a brother to James. Again, not definitive, but a strong clue that this isn't our author.

The author does not seem to be the apostle Jude, *son* of James, of number two, for the author seems to separate himself from the original apostles in verse 17. Not definitive, but a strong clue that this isn't our author.

Judas of Damascus in number three plays a part in the church's story, but is nowhere mentioned other than his house was the place where Saul of Tarsus spent three days fasting and praying after he saw the light and prior to his discussion with Ananias and his immersion into Christ. Again, not definitive, but a strong clue that this isn't our author.

I personally believe (and maybe you do, too) that the author of the letter bearing his name was the brother of the

Lord, and, therefore, brother of the James who figured in as very prominent in the early Jerusalem church which we have recorded in Acts chapter 15. If the Jude that wrote this letter is indeed the brother of Jesus, then there is a great lesson to be learned in verse one alone--to feel one's place as a bondservant of Jesus Christ is more important than either kinship ties or apostolic ties. If I grew up with Jesus as my older brother, I would be tempted to wear it out on my sleeve for all to see. That distinction would most certainly be listed on my résumé or CV! How about you?

We look at that lesson and say, "Sure," but how many times have we sat around discussing who knows who and who is related to what preacher, minister, priest or pastor and who preached where we attended and who had an uncle that was a shepherd in what church (not to mention the size of the church!)--not for the sake of digging up old friends or discovering who may know who, but for the sake of one-upping the other through association? Psychologists and counselors have a name for this and I'll leave it to them to explain. Just remember, Jude opted to do no such thing. He counted discipleship as the highest title of all. End of lesson 1.

At times we need lesson 1.

Although some men of the Reformation Movement, such as Martin Luther and John Calvin, argued against the letter of Jude as having a place in the Bible (they really did--along with James' letter), it was to be found in the Bible list, or canon, of the Synod of Laodicea in 363 AD (Calvin and Luther argued for and against quite a number of things that just ain't so). The letter of Jude was accepted by Origen as far back as the beginning of the second century and the Muratorian Canon of 170 AD (one of the earliest Bible lists) includes the book of Jude. Lesson 2: Jude is part of the Bible. It may be short, but it belongs.

The main argument against the authenticity of this letter is the references to the two apocryphal works (like Revelation & Ezekiel) named the *Assumption of Moses* and the *Book of Enoch*. Both of these works belong to a class of writing known by scholars as a pseudepigraphical (what?) writing, a Greek superword that simply means "books with false titles." This was a popular type of writing during the time in, around and between *Malachi* and *Matthew* for both those of Jewish decent and others.

Here's how the pseudepigraphi-*whatever* writings worked: moral messages were written and then names of historically famous or otherwise important people of a much earlier period were given as authors to enhance the authority and legitimacy of the work--therefore, a pseudepigrapha. No one was trying to 'put one over' on the readers, it was just the way it was done. This argument will be dealt with as the two references appear in the text in the body of the commentary. Never forget that although the authors of the various books of both the Old and New Testaments were inspired, God did not take away their style. This is why Mark and Luke don't have look-alike gospels. This is why Luke is in chronological order and Matthew is in, well, Jewish order.

The general feeling among those today who hold that the Bible is the inspired word of God is that the letter from Jude does indeed belong among the ranks of the rest of the Old and New Testament. Outside of a small group of theologians who seem hell-bent on watering down the scriptures, there is no question as to Jude's place in the Bible. One item to keep in mind is this: one must read Jude for themselves and decide if it is from God or from man. If one decides it is from man's mind only, then there will be very little gained from reading it. If one decides that it is from God, then a decision will have to be made. In Acts chapter 5, a wise man named Gamaliel said something along these lines. Start in verse 17 and finish that particular chapter. Amazing insight!

I do find it creepily ironic while trying to flesh this out from a seminary (and hopefully seminal) assignment, that Jude is the patron saint of desperate cases and lost causes. If this book is a lost cause, so be it. However, don't let your Christian walk and your local church be a lost cause. The stakes are too high.

Recipients of Jude

The letter of Jude was written to "those who are called" and, just like the author, little more can be realized with any certainty, without conjecture. We can, however, know something about the condition of the church that Jude was addressing, and this will be discussed under the section Occasion and Purpose. I don't know about you, but I sometimes get tickled in a Sunday school or Bible class setting where 50% or more of class time can be taken up discussing and hashing about who it was that received Jude, Ephesians, James and others. Again, it was "Those who are called." I get tickled at other things in Bible class, but those stories will hold for another time.

We have the recipients of the personal epistles, or letters, spelled out for us in the opening verses such as Luke's gospel, Acts, Titus, Timothy, Philemon, or Timothy's younger brother Second Timothy. City or regional epistles such as Romans, First and Second Peter, or Colossians are also spelled out for us. Although we do not have the original recipients of Jude preserved for us today, we can be assured that the Holy Spirit designed this letter, not only for the church of Jude's day, but for us who are called two thousand years later, as well.

As one begins to read this or any letter of the Bible, much will be gained if the honest thought at the onset is, "This letter was written to me for a specific purpose *at this point in my life*, so that I may walk closer with my God." If we add the phrase *at this point in my life* each time we study, we gain fresh insights from the mind of God. This is what Paul meant in Second Timothy 3:16*ff*. The Bible is meant to change the life of the one who reads it. It has been doing that for thousands of years and can continue to do so.

The Hebrew writer stated that the Word of God was, is, and will always be active--alive! No matter our age, our state, our mound of possessions or debt--the Word fits.

Occasion and Purpose of Jude

There are many preparatory things that we can do to enhance our study of the Bible and individual books and subjects. I believe that a study of the occasion and purpose of any letter or general writing is a first step and a must in gaining a greater insight into the meaning and the overall lesson it contains. It is no more than the answer to the great question of why a letter was written. We do this with *Reader's Digest* and *Time* articles, but sometimes fail to answer the occasion and purpose question with our Bibles. Ouch! For example, when we discover why *Gulliver's Travels* was written, due to the political clime of the time, the book becomes ever so much more delightful and insightful. When we discover why nursery rhymes were coined, they cease to be simply children's jingles, and the irony and sarcasm can almost be transferred to our day and time. Without the background, Gulliver and Mother Goose are fun--just not as much so. The Bible books are no different, whether they be letter, history, prophecy or prediction. When we have the background, occasion and purpose of each book or section of scripture (Lk 18:9), the meanings come alive.

Generally, all churches in Palestine and Asia Minor were being attacked by false teachers during the apostolic age, as they certainly are today, everywhere and in every city. Anywhere there is truth, falsehood will not be far behind. One needs only to read the Book of Acts to see that as soon as truth was delivered to a city, almost immediately within a few verses there was a caravan of false teachers arriving on the very heels of the evangelist to try to put things back the way they were! True then, true now. Nothing has changed in that regard. Satan isn't taking a nap somewhere because a new century and generation has come to be. Judaizers may not enter your church building on the following Sunday insisting on circumcision and animal sacrifices, but rest assured that Satan will try, try, try to move in false teaching--or keep one there.

For the first century disciples, it began with Judaizers who held allegiance to the Law of Moses in a legalistic way (trying their hardest to resist change. Sound familiar?) and slowly developed and morphed into Gnosticism. I would have to double this book in size and price if I tried to explain all of the ins and outs of Gnosticism. You can readily study the whole thing out through your church library or a simple Wiki jaunt, but let me state that Gnosticism is really just another form of rationalized legalism when you flip it over and examine its soft underbelly. Jude felt it necessary to defend the faith that had been delivered to the church.

Because this letter was written in a time when the church, though still in its infancy, was into the second and possibly third generations of disciples, faith may have simply become a tradition and not a reality. You know full well what is meant here: "Mom, why do we *hafta* go to church today?" "Well, because it's Sunday, *that's* why!" Whatever the specific occasion was, Jude felt it was necessary to place on hold his first intentions to write--important a subject as it was--so as to be able to hit the problem head on.

Jude felt his letter was much needed to fight off the heresy that was creeping into the church. He cited examples of ungodliness and the judgment thereof, and applied them to the church in his day. The first theme of Jude's letter that surfaces is, "God has, and will always, condemn evil doers. "

A secondary theme of Jude is that toleration is not a Christian virtue when it comes to false, and therefore damaging, teaching. I often wonder where the church would be today if toleration had been indeed stopped in the first century when the Bible writers were calling for its halt. We can only wonder.

Allow me some time here on this phenomenon of toleration. The church of God must make up her mind on this. The world (i.e. Satan... remember him?) cries for toleration and cries out when it finds one not playing by the world's rules. Notice I said the *world's* rules. I'm not writing about the petty squabbles that churches get into, bashing each other over items such as pianos, missionary endeavors, Bible versions or the layout of the Sunday morning worship. Again, *world's* rules.

What does the world cry out about? Everyone is the same. Nothing is inherently wrong or right, it simply just is. Religion shouldn't try to change folks, just include them. Contrast the world's rules with God's. God himself is not tolerant. He might be patient beyond our wildest imagination, but he is not tolerant. His word is truth and His words are the standard. Sin, on the other hand, is just that and is a violation of the standard. God, in numerous places in both the Old and New Testaments, calls for an immediate cessation of toleration, and calls folks to imitate Him. The world calls that politically incorrect. When hopping off the fence, we must decide which side to hop onto.

Again, Satan doesn't take us by demon possession, scary as that may seem. Why waste the effort and tie up demons here and there? For crying out loud, it took several thousand demons to subdue the poor fellow in Mark chapter 5. Besides, as we've noted before, that's just not good public relations to advertise yourself like that. No, demon possession just wouldn't work in our time zone and culture. He's got us, by and large, by other means. We're held in check by material possession, while we follow the world's world view.

We tend to agree with the world who cries out to us to simply accept and love and nurture everyone just where they are, and not hint at the fact that God calls them to change. We are told not to change a thing with anyone, for who knows, we just might have a log in our own eye. Who knows, God might just have made them that way, and for a reason. We're asked by the world not to ever, ever criticize without first walking a mile or five in someone's moccasins. Brethren, assisting someone in ferreting out sin in their life is not being critical, it is being biblical. I've sung the song *Just As I Am* a gozillion times. It has a lot of verses. A lot. I do not recall one of the verses saying:

> *Just as I am, Just little ol' me;*
> *Don't ask me to change, I like being me.*
> *I know you want me to be-come Thine,*
> *O Lamb of God, I'm fine, I'm fine!*

Don't get me wrong about toleration. I'm not for the horrendous way the church in the past has insisted that one 'cleans up their life' in order to become a follower of Jesus. I'm not for laying down rules for folks just to let them into the church building. We are to love the sinner, hate the sin, and walk with the sinner to bring them to God and His ways. This was Jesus while He was with us on earth. This was the Jesus who was looked at with suspicion in the first two verses of Luke chapter 15 by the leading religious folks of His day. This is what Jesus was trying to get us to understand when He told us of the lost sheep, the lost coin and the lost son, as Luke continued writing in verse three when he wrote these words, "And he told them this parable, saying..."

For no extra charge, since we're still in the Occasion and Purpose section, Luke 15:1-2 is both the occasion and purpose for verses 3 through the end of that chapter of the lost sheep, lost coin and the lost son. Neat, huh?

As far as the church being into possibly the third generation and tradition settling in, think about how that plays out today. Often times we find ourselves as a body of believers going through the motions of our Sunday ritual. To be sure, the devotion is there for the most part. Because we become creatures of habit does not demand that our devotion to God fly out the window. I, for one, am tired of being told that it does. How 'bout you? However, if we do not pass that devotion along to the next generation (which does not necessarily have to be our individual children) we run the risk of passing along tradition only. Tradition, under those circumstances, will surely become set into cement. That we do something a certain way isn't wrong, if it is according to the Scriptures. That we run the risk of doing it in a rote way, void of the heart, is no better than what Jesus was talking about in Mark chapter 7, not to mention missing the message of Micah 6:6-8.

Again, please take the time to read the Bible references.

Date and Place of Writing of Jude

Nothing can be concluded with any certainty concerning the date and the origin of the letter, for none is given in the letter itself. If Jude were the brother of the Lord, then one cannot stretch the date too far past the close of the first century without stretching the age of the man Jude. Most serious Bible scholars place the writing of Jude at sometime between the years 65-95 AD. One could possibly date the epistle from several events involving the first century church. We assume Paul's death at the hands of Nero to be most likely 64 to 67 AD from tradition. Other apostles' deaths, except for James the son of Zebedee (Acts 12), are not spoken of in Scripture either and can only be speculated about through tradition. Hebrews seems to have been written after all of the apostles' deaths (Heb 2:3*f*) but before the destruction of Jerusalem at the hands of the Roman general Titus (Heb 10:25) in the year 70 AD. Jude makes no mention or allusion to the collapse of Jerusalem and, therefore, Judaism as a way of life, so it may be safe to date the epistle at the late sixties. In fact, it just may be the last book to have been written. I know that Revelation is last in placement. However, it was written before First John. It really was! But, that is for another time.

More than likely, Jude was living in or around the city of Jerusalem and penned the letter from there, for we know that the apostles and the early church leaders stayed in Jerusalem when the church was scattered early on (Act 8:1) in her existence. But for us today, neither the date nor the author of the epistle of Jude carries with it the importance that the content of the letter does as it speaks to us today.

Unique Features of Jude

Some writers and teachers feel, because of the similarity of Second Peter chapter 2, that either Jude copied from the apostle Peter, or Peter copied from Jude. Indeed, there are many similarities between the two pieces of inspired literature, but we must not speak of one writer copying from another at the expense of inspiration, since the Bible is very clear on itself concerning inspiration (II Tim 3:16). One must also consider that Jude was written after the deaths of the Lord's apostles. This would not be copying in a negative sense, but would be the same as the admonition Paul gave the Philippian church in Philippians 3:1, "To write the same things again is no trouble to me, and it is a safeguard for you." If you want a real rush, read the last two verses of Second Chronicles and the first three verses of Ezra. Many of the Proverbs are repeated, just in case we didn't get it the first time! Jesus preached the same sermons on more than one occasion (just as many of us do today). Read the Gospels carefully.

One proposal that has validity (but no proof as to claim certainty) states that Jude wrote to the same recipients that Second Peter was addressed to, which were the churches of Galatia, Cappadocia, Pontus, Bithynia, and Asia (I Pet 1:1 & II Pet 3:1). Look at the Bible map in the back of your Bible and see if that isn't a pretty hefty chunk of first century real estate. Second Peter was written as a warning that false prophets would arise, and Jude wrote to tell them they were indeed *there in the church already perched on the front pews and singing loudly.* (II Pet 2:1 & Jude v.4). This may account for the parallelism that exists between much of the body of Jude and the second chapter of Second Peter. This is not without problems, however, for Jude seems to have been written to a specific body of believers (or at least a limited region) and

Peter wrote to an area covering over 262,000 square miles--roughly the size of Texas! No matter the conclusion, it would be time well spent to read Second Peter chapter 2 at this point. (meaning, yes, read II Pet 2 at this point).

C'mon, guys!

Unlike Peter, Jude makes use of the triplet or literary triad. This is simply a listing of items, attributes or descriptions in sets of three. I might say of my work, "I work, slave and toil all week," so I quit my job and go to the Mojave which is hot, dry and dead with all the plants that either poke, scratch or stick you. In First Corinthians chapter 13, Paul states, "But now abide faith, hope, love, these three; but the greatest of these is love."

In Jude there are twelve triads in all, six of which fall closely together in verses by themselves. The original language of this letter (a regional Greek called *koine*) is rich and diverse in vocabulary with historical references from the Old Testament, indicating that these original recipients were at least well versed in Jewish history, or expected to be so. That same Old Testament that we have at our disposal. Jude is reproachful in nature and filled with warnings for both the ungodly and those under their influence. I repeat, it is filled with warnings for both the ungodly and those under their influence. The overall pace of the letter is quick and the nature of the tone is severe. It would seem that Jude wanted his letter out--quickly! The Holy Spirit wanted it to stay out--for us, a few years down the road.

And He wanted it read.

The author minces no words in both his pronouncement of judgment from God and his ending plea to give assistance to those who struggle under the strain of the false teachers who have crept in unnoticed into this particular body, or region, of believers. I wonder just how many sermons like this would folks sit through before they said something to the preacher?

After reading the last few paragraphs on the nature and tone of the letter from Jude, I also wonder just how well this type of letter would be received today in the true church of the Lord? I'm not talking about religious outfits that are more concerned with shallow hoop-de-doo form above function so folks can get a religious buzz on Sunday morning that wears off by Monday, but true churches who strives to teach and live according to the principles set forth in God's word. At the writing of this paragraph during a draft revision, I had just recently watched a television program in which an ordained reverend from a high fired theological center for higher learning was consulted on a matter of Christianity. Leaving out the main question, his answer clearly stated that he thought that what was wrong with the church today was her intoleration of non- and anti-Christian religions and the ungodly choices that people make in their lives. He stated plainly that for too long the church has rested on a God centered theology and we need to now shift onto a man centered theology. He offered that to make just a few minor adjustments in the area of inclusion and toleration, that the church would *get back on track* and fly forward through the 21st century. God through Jude didn't have the same idea. Do we? We are now most certainly flying through that 21st century. The TV prediction, by and large, has come true with some. We're certainly better at inclusion and toleration, but it is killing the church.

The Outline

While there are many time honored outlines for Jude, the following outline will be followed for the remainder of this book. In looking back on this outline, I'm not real sure what use and purpose it serves for the majority reading this little work. It will certainly be helpful if one is to teach the letter of Jude. For sure, I was not going to receive a passing grade without it!

I. Introduction to Jude (vs 1-4)
   A. Greeting (vs 1-2)
   B. Occasion and Purpose (vs 3-4)
      • Men crept in unnoticed by the church
      • They were not unnoticed by God
II. Ungodliness Will Receive the Judgment of God (vs 5-16)
   A. Examples of Old Testament Judgment (vs 5-11)
      • Upon Egypt
      • Upon Angels
      • Upon the Cities of the Plain
      • Upon Individual Rebels
   B. Judgment Pronounced on Evil Today (vs 12-16)
      • Men's evil hidden from the church
      • They will not be unnoticed by God
III. Christians Will Escape the Wrath of God (vs 17-25)
   A. The Christian Can Shun Evil Through the Word (vs 17-23)
      • Leaning on the Apostles' teachings
      • Leaning on the power of prayer
      • Leaning on the spiritually strong
   B. God Works in the Christian Through Christ (vs 24-25)
      • Christ is the leaning post
      • Christ is our only anchor into eternity

And so, there you have it. An outline for whatever purpose an outline of Jude will serve. Again, this is the outline that will be followed in the commentary part of this work, the Roman numerals standing as the divisions.

The Commentary

The following is a verse by verse commentary on Jude. The text quoted is the New American Standard version of the Bible. The verses themselves have been inserted for ease of study, however, I strongly recommended that you keep an open Bible handy for other references. The word studies and overall commentary sections were gathered in part from several decades of studying and teaching Jude and other books of the Bible. I say in part, for also they were in part gathered at the feet of many a fine instructor during my tenure at Bible Boot Camp and many fine preachers of the gospel plus the aid of other writers. The short sermons interspersed are mine to aid one in drawing out the meaning and application of this beautiful short epistle into life. In short, even though there is no bibliography at the end, I am not original. No one is. However God is and however we might rightly aid the spread of His word, He will be glorified. Let's study Jude.

Oops, one last thing. Have you read Jude in its entirety and prayed about it? If not, why not? We've got to become, once again, a people of the Book. Once Dee and I were visiting someone during a break at Sunset. One evening, we stayed up late discussing one or more aspects of the Bible. We weren't fussing and feuding and getting our feathers ruffled, just having a discussion about God and His word. We were quoting Scripture and (hopefully not mis-) applying it to the conversation. Our host got stumped along the way on her side of the discussion and soon it was time to go to bed. The next day our host was at work and was relating this discussion to one of her coworkers and related the fact that we, "really knew our way around the Bible." When asked what flavor we were, she told them (but I'm not telling you :-). "Oh, no need to get into a discussion with them," the coworker said, "They know their Bibles!" I appreciate the pat on the head, but I wonder just how true that is today. It is time for Christians to come back to that challenge and description. It is time for us, like the shepherd king, David, to hide God's word in our heart that we might not sin against Him (Ps 119).

Introduction to Jude, vs 1-4

I didn't write Jude. Jude did. Part of me deep down wants to skip over verses 1-4, quickly scan verses 5-16 and land squarely on the first word of verse 17, "But..."Why? Because of what those last nine verses hold: *hope for the hurting, sometimes doubting disciple of Christ.* Indeed, it is very much hoped that many picked up this book in the first place because that concept was put forth on the cover.

However, Jude wrote Jude and had the added bonus of THE Editor-in-Chief! I truly believe that when we do reach the last section of this powerful letter of warning and hope, that those who do seek help in their daily walk will understand why Jude is written in the order it is in.

V.1 Jude, a bondservant of Jesus Christ, and brother of James, to those who are the called, beloved in God the Father, and kept for Jesus Christ:

In this greeting, or salutation (vs 1-2), we see the author identifying himself by use of the first of the dozen triads, or literary triplets. His name is Jude, he is a bondservant of Christ and brother of James. The term bondservant, or slave (Greek *doulos*), that Jude describes himself as, is a characteristic description of the followers of Christ and is included in many salutations and other passages (Romans, Titus, James, II Peter). He addresses the letter to the called, as disciples are called through the gospel (II Thess 2:14 & John 6:41-45). We can note again that even though the specific recipients are lost to us, we know that he is most certainly writing to the elect of God, therefore, we know that this letter transcends time and lands in our lap--it is written to us, the church of today. If you are called (past tense), Jude is for you, today. If you have not been called, listen carefully. Jesus is calling you right now. He has been and will continue to do so.

The phrases beloved in God the Father, and kept for Jesus Christ, denote the status of the disciple of Christ after his calling through the gospel. We are not hung out to dry and left to do the best that we can here on earth. We're given the promise by Jesus himself in John chapter 10 that we sit in His hand and no one can snatch us out.

Many reading this book will remember a certain television program when I throw out the phrase, "Grasshopper, snatch this pebble from my hand." The blind Shaolin Master would hold out his hand, complete with pebble, and young Kwai Chang Caine would try each week to snatch it. He couldn't. In illustrating the promise that we sit in the hand of God and no one can snatch us out, I decided to try this one Sunday. In the middle of the sermon I challenged one from the youth group to try and snatch the pebble. She promptly did. I wasn't quite ready so I pled do-overs. She promptly snatched it again and I promptly told her to sit back down. I tried another teen. Pebble went sailing across the sanctuary, bounced off of Sister Mabel's head, and rolled under a pew.

But I'm not God. Nowhere near. Evidently, I'm not a blind Shaolin Master, either. But, think again about the promise of John chapter 10. Think on what Jude is telling us as God's kids, that we are kept for Jesus Christ. God doesn't require do-overs. He doesn't need to warm up. He doesn't fumble us under the church house pew. Rest assured, brother or sister, that you are safe in the hand of Jesus the Christ. Now THAT is some big promise. Disciples are richly fed each day by the Spirit of God--if we so choose. We will be, by and large, what we eat. The question is, "What do you eat?"

V.2 May mercy and peace and love be multiplied to you.

In the second verse of this greeting we see Jude's wish for the recipients in the form of a third triplet (verse one held two triads). All three of these blessings come from God and the writer wishes that they be multiplied to the readers. As people (especially Christian people), we are capable of dispensing all three of these blessings to each other from time to time, however, with surety any church of God which is undergoing the problems that Jude will shortly expose will need mercy, peace, and love in unending quantities--not just from the brethren, but from the throne room of God. I honestly believe that this is more than just the way they used to start letters back then. These three items are God's gifts to His kids. When we think about it, without any of these three items we will simply not complete our Christian walk here on earth and certainly never see Heaven's Gate.

Maybe next time that you bow your head at the dinner table or stand before your church family at the microphone next Sunday, you start your prayer by thanking God for His mercy, peace, and love in unending quantities. You just might get someone tilting their head up and cracking an eye to see just who it is that is praying! Without these three qualities, we are dead in the waters of life.

Before Jude addresses the occasion and purpose of the letter and the problem that he wishes to expose, he shows his genuine concern for those involved through the salutation. It is my studied opinion that these greetings go far beyond that which is customary (and that view of 'customary' is probably why we jump over the greetings at times to get into the 'meat' of the letter!). Even the polemic letter to the Galatians contains a similar greeting as Paul shows his concern for straying disciples. Take the time to turn back and read Galatians 1:3 to see what I mean. It may be a lesson well learned to imitate these types of greetings, especially when we are getting ready to 'really give one' to a brother or sister. We might just keep our brother or sister.

In order for us to dispense mercy, peace and love to each other, we must truly be selfless. I can't give you mercy if I am egocentric. You can't give me love if you are the center of your universe. Peace will not prevail in a church family if we are all acting like individual planets wandering aimlessly about our own galaxies. We sing *Father of Mercies*, *Peace, Perfect Peace*, and *Love One Another*. We must be willing to go beyond singing about them. Remember, we cannot tell someone to be warmed and be filled. We've got to hand them a blanket and a bag of groceries.

V.3 Beloved, while I was making every effort to write you about our common salvation, I felt the necessity to write to you appealing that you contend earnestly for the faith which was once for all delivered to the saints.

Jude begins his occasion by addressing the church as beloved, a term which was common in the apostolic writings and continues the genuine concern that was shown in verse 2. Again, a lesson for us today. As was noted in the Occasion and Purpose, the overall pace of the letter is quick and the tone is severe in nature. There are times in the church when dealing with brothers and sisters that our speech and writing (read: e-mails) must be the same. However, I wonder just how much more our comments and warnings would be taken to heart if we started out our confrontations with one another using the word beloved. Perhaps they would be a little less confrontational and more for the building up of one another.

If you are new to the idea of one another, or it has become hazy during your Christian walk, there are many books on the subject. One of them is mine, however, it is a concept that must be learned and taken to heart in our walk here on this earth.

It is not known by what means that Jude learned of the condition of the church, but upon learning he put aside what he had intended to write concerning their common salvation and felt the need of addressing the problem at hand. Take a moment and stop and thank God for the tattle tales in the church (I Cor 1:11)! "Yes, but they tell on us!!!" Yep, they do, but thank God for them just the same.

We must remember that writing in the first century was still a great undertaking compared to today's computer age. Indeed, scrounging up some parchment and ink just might have been the effort that Jude was making in order to write about the common salvation. I often wonder just what Jude was going to say on that matter. I'll ask him when I see him. I'll pass it on to you when you get there.

We can learn from this imperative that the faith is indeed something that can be contended for, and this should be done in an earnest fashion, seriously and intently. Jude is not resorting to today's yellow journalism that seems to pervade the brotherhood (by that I mean being contentious for the faith instead of contending for it!) especially through the internet medium. Neither is he appealing to a mixture of faith and subjectivism that would change from location to location and from time period to time period (becoming increasingly popular in today's sermonettes), but rather to a doctrine that was delivered to the saints. This message is important today as man looks around and experiences many flashing neon signs that proclaim 'truth' but little resemble either the church as Christ intended it to be or the Scriptures that were left as a pattern for eternal life in Christ. Maybe it is a fair question to ask you if you believe that there is a pattern for Christianity? If your answer is yes, read on. If your answer is no, then there is nothing to contend for and you can quietly put this little work down. Sorry for the cost.

Jude recognizes that all who have participated in the gospel of Christ are saints, and they are not a special group of disciples set apart from the rest of Christ's body (I Cor 1:2 & Heb 6:10). One does not have to do some strange, miraculously wondrous or otherwise weird thing in life--and then die--in order to become a saint. Saints were meant to be saved live folk first, then continue as such after death (Rev 6:9*ff*). I once was having a discussion about this or that with one of my deacons. In reference to something he stated, "Well, I'm no saint, but..." I quickly replied, "Then accept Jesus and let me baptize you into Christ." He looked at me rather dumbfounded and said, "What are you talking about? I'm a Christian, I'm just saying I'm not a saint..." I offered again to baptize him into Christ. He probably still thinks I'm a nut, but we've got to grasp as Christians that we are saints while we're working here on earth out of branch offices, and will still be saints after we receive our transfer to the home office!

V.4 For certain persons have crept in unnoticed, those who were long beforehand marked out for this condemnation, ungodly persons who turn the grace of our God into licentiousness and deny our only Master and Lord, Jesus Christ.

The word *for* cues us as to the reason that Jude felt it necessary to write the epistle. The word *certain* (Greek indefinite pronoun TIS) may give us some insight into what group Jude was writing about. This indefinite pronoun is used of persons or things that the writer either cannot or will not speak about more particularly in many instances, as may be the case in the epistle of Jude. In other occurrences the person or place is identified. We have but to see how it is used in the rest of the Scriptures, for example Luke chapter 10, to form the idea that Jude may have written his epistle to a particular church with specific, yet unnamed persons in mind (though their positional relationship to the body will be explored later) leading us to believe that by the time the letter is finished, they knew who these folks were! With that said, let me show you an example of the word we translate as certain.

In Luke 10:38, Jesus enters a certain village, and a certain woman welcomed Him into her home. That woman is identified as Martha, but the village of Bethany is not named in this passage (Jno 11:1 & 12:1).

Luke 10:25, And behold a certain lawyer stood up and put Him to the test... Whereupon Jesus answered the lawyer with a story concerning a certain man who fell among robbers, and a certain Samaritan who helped him. Although no one's name is given in this story, their occupations or nationalities are, no one argued with Jesus and the story's lesson was understood.

I'm not a betting man, but if I were, I'd betcha a dollar to a donut that the certain lawyer either knew the certain man who fell among robbers or the certain Samaritan that helped him. Or could it be that he knew the other players in the incident--the ones with blinders on? Scary thought, when you think about the possibilities. Was he traveling with one of the players with blinders on? For the Lawyer's sake, I hope not.

In the book of Jude, the recipients simply are not named, but the Greek word for certain may help us conclude that this epistle was intended to be a specific one at its writing, but that the original destination is lost to us at this point in history.

And I'm actually glad that Jude didn't name anyone specifically. Human nature being what it is, if Jude had done so it might not carry the same weight with us today. What would we do, for instance, if Jude had written, "For Sam and Dave have crept in unnoticed..."? Every time that we sat down to read Jude today we would think harshly about ol' Sam and Dave, long dead, and perhaps never notice that the same thing was creeping in and around us today in our church local. Just a thought.

Condemnation had been sentenced upon men of this kind by that which had previously been written (II Pet 2:1-3). The grace of our God is salvation (Eph 2:8*f*), and these men were turning it into licentiousness. The word licentiousness in its simpler form can mean outrageousness and shamelessness, but can include indecent behavior of men and women with each other, or lust. Thus in behaving this way, they deny our only Master and Lord, Jesus Christ. How could this be? How can a shameful behavior possibly deny Jesus as Lord?

To be sure, these men were holding to the Gnostic thought that Jesus didn't really come in the flesh, but spirit only. Here's a little further insight into that thought: Jesus came in spirit only because spirit is good and flesh is bad, therefore, we might as well do anything (read: *anything!*) we want to do in the flesh because flesh is unredeemable and we should only pay attention to our spirit so lust away just don't forget to mark up Heaven points by praying, giving... See what I meant about Gnosticism under Occasion and Purpose? Rationalized legalism.

I know, I know, it sounds crazy but anytime we rationalize our lives and allow sin to come in, it is both crazy and will deny our only Master and Lord, Jesus Christ. Christians should be both a *say* AND a *do* people. This was the whole point of Jesus' question, "And why do you *call* me 'Lord, Lord,' and *do not do* what I say?"

It is a lesson for all who hold their Lord dear and strive to live like the Master that our actions and our ways of life are only manifestations of our attitudes and what is in our heart. Attitudes are not created in a vacuum, but created by our will. Attitudes certainly cannot be hidden from God and cannot stay hidden from other folks, within or without the church. Sooner or later our attitudes will come out in our actions!

And when they are the wrong attitudes, it results in total embarrassment!--it should.

But someone may well cry out, "Surely, Jude isn't writing about any type of sexual connotation, is he?! That's just too way out for me to imagine! How could something like THAT even take place in a church setting?!" Remember, in its simplest form licentiousness can mean outrageous or shameless--but not always. Folks, it does happen. On November 18, 1978, near the equator in a small South American country, 918 people lay dead after drinking cyanide-laced punch. They had started out as a church. By their end, they were anything but.

Use an internet search engine and search insurance claims against church misconduct and see what you come up with. Thank goodness most are just reports and not convictions. However, it does show just where a church can go if the leaders lead in that particular direction, or allow themselves, unchecked by the flock, to slip into the depths of depravity. How does it get stopped and corrected? Through a thorough understanding and adherence to the Word of God, spiritual maturity. That adherence to the Word of God must come through a deep devotion to God and His ways.

Jude tells us in verse 4 that to take a left turn and lead a church away from the teachings of God is paramount to one who would *deny our only Master and Lord, Jesus Christ.* Many years ago I pulled a quote out of Norman Hogan's book, *Leadership in the Local Church*, and wrote it in the front of my Bible. It reads:

If members of a local church refuse to lead for Christ, it is certain that others, whose philosophy of life is alien to that of Christians, will lead people away from Christ

This was true in Jude's day, and true in ours.

Ungodliness Will Receive the Judgment of God, verses 5-16

I didn't write Jude. Jude did. We're entering a section of the letter that may sound utterly fantastic to some. Actually, it does to me every time I read it. We want to ask the question, "*How in the world* can something like this even remotely happen in the church of our Lord?!" The answer is in the question: *in the world*.

Think about how distasteful this must have been to Jude as he wrote this letter. Then think about how distasteful this was to God, as He saw these disrupters tearing apart the very body that He went to the cross for.

V.5 Now I desire to remind you, though you know all things once for all, that the Lord, after saving a people out of the land of Egypt, subsequently destroyed those who did not believe.

Jude is not going to give the recipients any new information, but simply wants to remind them of what has already been delivered, as we read in verse 3. The reference to the Old Testament recordings of the destruction of the Israelites who were in the exodus from Egypt parallels First Corinthians 10:1-11. Jude reminds them that the reason they were destroyed is because of unbelief. Wow, now THAT sentence probably turned some heads when it was read out loud. We can pause and look back at the first four verses of the epistle and see the wisdom that Jude used in wording those verses. How would the church have received his letter if it started out with verse five? One verse in the New Testament that I have preached entire sermons on is found in Colossians 4:6 and is worth preaching on here:

Let your speech always be with grace, seasoned as it were, with salt, so that you may know how you should respond to each person.

We spend a lot of time and energy worrying about the what: what to say to folks when we talk with them about their eternal soul. This verse ain't concerned with the *what*. It is concerned with the *how*. Did you see it? The verse states, "...so that you will know how you should respond..." The *what* is important. Deathly important. So is the *how*. Deathly so. If we don't get the *how* right, we'll never get the *what* out of our mouths, for folks will be through with us. We will turn them off and they won't listen. Even though Jude had a true, yet harsh, warning to give to these brethren, he got the how done right. The warning is clear and the theme of the epistle stands out: God will punish those who are unfaithful. Who are the unfaithful today?

So often, faithfulness and church attendance are used interchangeably. I'm not sure where or how we arrived at this, but often we see it this way. Jesus was very clear on this matter when He finished two very similar sounding sermons with the parable of the wise and foolish builders. Take the time next Monday at lunch to read the Sermon on the Mount in Matthew chapters five through seven, and the Sermon on the Plains in Luke chapter six. Jesus says in one place, "Not everyone who says to me, 'Lord, Lord.'" and in the other He clearly asks, "And why do you call me, 'Lord, Lord,' and do not do what I say?" To be sure, the faithful will gather with the saints. To be equally sure, gathering with the saints is not paramount with salvation. Sitting in a hen house doesn't make you eligible to lay eggs! You can sit there day after day cackling with chicken goo and feathers stuck all over you, flapping your arms, but there won't be an egg one underneath you. Sitting in a pew doesn't make you eligible for Heaven, either. Faithfulness is much, much more, going far beyond Sunday morning from 10 AM to noon.

Many of the great Bible doctrines that mankind has held dear through the centuries has come to us by way of reminders. For examples in the New Testament see First Corinthians 15:3 (the core of the good news), Romans 6:3 ("Or do you not know" meaning "I know you know"), and the greater part of the epistle of Philippians (3:1). Often Jesus would answer those who were trying to trip Him up with trick questions, by reaching back into Genesis for an answer (Matt 19:1-6). In our teaching of one another both the words of Christ and the ways of Christ, we need to remember the 3-R's of a disciple's learning: repetition, repetition, repetition.

Sometimes, we as human beings become addicted to something new. Hamburger joints must constantly put out a new 'Cajun BBQ Double Fish Megawich' in order to keep us coming back. Clothing designers must keep changing pockets, belt loops, labels and colors to keep us buying the latest jeans. When it is all over and the dust has settled, we still have just a fish sandwich and a pair of pants. However, like Dr. Seuss' Sneetches, we are never satisfied until we have stamped on, and removed off, the 'stars upon thars' a million times.

I saw this over and over in counseling sessions I would hold. Couples, individuals, parents and children, all wanting something new and improved for their situation (I Cor 10:13). More often than not, the answer was something old: stop being selfish, put others first, watch your mouth, shower regularly and humble yourself before God. More often than not, the answers were rejected. We're hooked on something new. Here, Jude gives them something old. Not old and worn out, but firmly entrenched as God's will and truth: God punishes the unfaithful.

Oh, and if you don't have a clue what I was talking about with Sneetches and stars and thars--go buy Dr. Seuess' *Sneetches and Other Stories*, especially if you are a church leader. Read it, understand it, and I guarantee a lot of church problems will disappear.

V.6 And angels who did not keep their own domain, but abandoned their proper abode, He has kept in eternal bonds under darkness for the judgment of the great day.

Angels. What a subject today! This, among other reasons, helps to keep this as one of the more difficult passages in the book of Jude. Critics of the authenticity of Jude believe that it references an uninspired apocryphal work titled *The Book of Enoch*. If Jude had referenced non-biblical works (and it sure looks like he did), we know that the Holy Spirit guided the writing of all the Old and New Testament alike, and this should pose no particular problem. We must keep in mind that it is possible, and is an everyday occurrence, that uninspired writers (a group which we fall into today) are capable of writing something that is authentic, true and reliable. Paul makes use of this in the Sermon on Mars Hill (Acts 17:28) and in writing to Titus in Crete (Tit 1:12*f*) about Cretans. Just because it didn't show up in the Old Testament doesn't make it untrue.

Let's explore another closely related incident just for fun. In James 5:17, James states that Elijah prayed that it might not rain. He prayed again in James 5:18 and it did rain. One can run up and down the book of First Kings and he won't find Elijah praying either for or against rain! We see him kneeling in First Kings 18:42, but it doesn't say he was praying. However, by inspiration through James, we know that prayer on the part of Elijah figured into the whole Ahab--dry spell--rain incident. And besides that, the story is just cool!

In Acts 20:35 Paul asked his listeners to "...remember the words of the Lord Jesus, that He Himself said, 'It is more blessed to give than to receive.'" We run up and down Matthew, Mark, Luke and John trying to find where Jesus said that. Did He say it? Yes. When did He say it? When He was here on earth teaching the masses and the disciples. Where, then, is it recorded for us? Acts 20:35.

Therefore, the difficulty lies with the scholars and not so much for the disciple. I think that's enough for this section. The horse is dead. Remove the saddle.

We have no way of knowing with certainty what it was that the angels did to deserve the eternal bonds of judgment. There's been much speculation, from the fall of Satan to a misapplication of Isaiah 14:12-15 (contextually applied to the king of Babylon, not Satan), but one should be careful to not be caught up in speculation at the expense of the lesson Jude is relating. We can be sure that whatever their proper abode was, God made that known to them. Like His dealings with us, God doesn't hide the rule book and then get tiffed when a rule is broken. God has always stated clearly what His will and expectation is for His creatures. Angels are God's creatures. God will not tolerate ungodliness and there will be a final judgment on those who did not keep their own domain, but abandoned their proper abode.

V.7 Just as Sodom and Gomorrah and the cities around them, since they in the same way as these indulged in gross immorality and went after strange flesh, are exhibited as an example, in undergoing the punishment of eternal fire.

This is again not a new teaching, but a reminder. The story of the destruction of the cities of the plain can be read in Genesis 18:16-19:29. What is noteworthy in this comparison is the fact that Jude says of the men in verse 4, since they in the same way as these indulged in gross immorality. As one rereads the wonderful account of the fall of Sodom and Gomorrah (hint, hint), he should keep in mind the men who were disrupting the church that Jude was addressing.

While it seems almost an impossibility that this type of immorality could exist in either a local congregation or a region today, we must not lose sight of the warning: if this could, and possibly did, exist in a church, how much harder to detect would a heresy of 'lesser' degree be to identify and subsequently ferret out? The cities of the plain, and likewise the church disrupters in the epistle, serve as an example of what befalls those who do not obey God (II Thess 1:8). Here again we are reminded that God has not become soft on sin somewhere between Malachi and Matthew. But maybe we have.

Look around in your local church today. Do you have anyone openly practicing fornication or deviant sexuality? Anyone tied to pornography? Anyone given over to substance abuse or addiction? Anyone openly and blatantly foul in their business practices? Anyone abusing their children or their mate? Chances are you will answer yes to any or all of the questions. Next set: Is the church doing anything about it, or is the church offering a guiding hand? Are they calling a sin a sin, and pleading with the sinner to change to God's ways? Are they turning their heads and saying, "Well, at least they come to church on Sundays?" Time tends to be a blinder. The longer something goes on, the more commonplace and familiar it becomes and the easier for something of greater degradation to slip in unnoticed. Sound familiar? Jude *is* for today!

V.8 Yet in the same manner these men, also by dreaming, defile the flesh, and reject authority, and revile angelic majesties.

Jude now fixes his attention to the men of verse four. These men live in a dream world and are legends in their own minds. We can clearly see their sins listed by way of one of Jude's triads. The sin of defiling the flesh is parallel to the passage in Romans 1:18-32. These men also reject authority, whether it be civil or religious (or, probably both), openly or in attitude, but probably on the grounds that the authority interferes with their own will. As human beings, we will come up with almost any excuse or rationalization technique when our own will is being violated, especially when our will is wrong.

Rejecting authority, whether it be religious or civil is to not hold to the standard. It is, in effect, lawlessness. Romans 13:1*f* is hard to carry out at times, but it's in the Bible. Note the warning that Jesus used in Matthew 7:21-23. It's not that they were (hey, did you read that passage?) doing bad things. It wasn't that they were not doing good things. It is that they rejected the standard either in part or the whole. Jesus says that this is lawlessness. It is to reject authority.

These men are guilty of the sin of reviling angelic majesties. The Greek word for *revile* is *blasphemeo* and is most generally transliterated (not translated) *blaspheme*. Its general meaning is to offer rash prayers or to speak profanely of something, usually a sacred item or person. The word *blaspheme* has been called here and there in books and sermons a genuine piece of Biblical Greek because it is a word which has acquired a technical meaning in association with Judaism and Christianity. In other words, catch the word *blaspheme* in a conversation and chances are you know it is a religious conversation.

Blasphemeo literally means *a judgment of railing*, but the beginning of the word is not certain. It may have derived from the Greek word *blaps* or *blabos*, which means *injurious speaking*, which best suits it etymologically, but this is not without difficulties in trying to pinpoint... You know what?...blah, blah, *blaps!* Who cares! With all that said, we still know what it means. It is usually a very dumb thing to blaspheme God, God's creation or God's kids. It's never a good word.

Other uses of this word in the New Testament include a

warning by Jesus to the scribes not to blaspheme against the Holy Spirit (Mk 3:28*ff*) without eternal consequences, and Paul's instruction to Timothy to teach slaves to honor their masters so that God's name and the Christian doctrine would not be blasphemed (I Tim 6:1). It's never a good word.

V.9 But Michael the archangel, when he disputed with the devil and argued about the body of Moses, did not dare pronounce against him a railing judgment, but said, "The Lord rebuke you."

This verse has been called by some scholars to be the most difficult verse in the entire New Testament. Take your pick out of some of these, however:
- Matthew 19:12
- I Peter 3:19
- I Timothy 2:15

What usually makes a verse difficult? Well, WE do. Oftentimes scholars, preachers and teachers use this 'difficult' phrase to hide behind because the verse takes work to understand; or it is at the core of an age old debate; or it will make the local church's biggest giver upset; or it simply dredges up too many emotions for the recipients. Ergo, we simply practice the passover and call it a difficult verse. Let's not call Jude 9 most difficult, rather let's plow through it the same as the rest of the letter.

Many scholars believe that Jude quotes from a pseudepigraphical work titled *The Assumption of Moses*, which exists only in fragment form today. This has caused some potholes for the epistle of Jude by waking up the naysayers. Again, what we must ever keep in mind is that Jude, an inspired writer--meaning guided by the Holy Spirit-- confirmed that the event did take place in history. Because Deuteronomy 34:6 does not include this confrontation between Michael and Satan, we must not conclude that it did not take place. Once again, I bring your attention back to James 5:17*f*. One may search First Kings over many times and not find the prayer of Elijah, yet James tells us that the supplication took place. First Kings 18:42 is certainly prayer position, but no record of prayer.

We are first introduced to Michael in Daniel 10:13, again in Jude, and finally in Revelation 12:7 where he wages war with Satan in the vision of John. He is an archangel, a term meaning a captain or chief angel. There are only two other angels in Scripture that we are given their names. I'm just sure the rest have names, but we aren't in on it. Maybe there is a Fred. We will all get introductions later when we get transferred to the home office. If you do indeed have a personal angel watching you, you'll get to meet him then. In the meantime, just try to follow God's Word.

The meaning of the verse is clear. If Michael, being an archangel, restrains from bringing a blasphemous judgment against the Devil but rather reserves that action for God, how much more unexcused were the false teachers when they blasphemed authority and angelic majesties and rejected them in Jude verse 8? Bottom line: Scripture speaks volumes about our mouths (many Proverbs, James 3, etc.) and the way we use it. Jesus said that what comes out of our mouths originates in our hearts (Mk 7). We know that all too well from experience!

V.10 But these men revile the things which they do not understand; and the things which they know by instinct, like unreasoning animals, by these things they are destroyed.

In verse 8, Jude tells the readers what the false teachers were doing and in verse 10 we are given insight as to why these men were blaspheming. They simply did not have an understanding insight into the heavenly realm or spiritual matters, therefore they revile the things which they do not understand. This is not to say that they were not given opportunity to understand, for that would be classified as the doctrine of election of a select few. Rather we are given the answer in the last half of the verse: *and the things which they know by instinct...by these things they are destroyed.* These things being the appetites and lusts of the flesh which was to their ultimate destruction. One sees God, not giving up on these men, but rather giving these men over to their own destruction because they did not receive the love of the truth so as to be saved (II Thess 2:11). Compare the lifestyle of these false teachers with those described by the apostle Paul in Romans chapter 1.

Again, it is very hard to imagine the church leaders succumbing to this type of behavior. However, if this is true then how much harder is it to ferret out those today who might be charged in a 'lesser' crime?

The underlying message of this verse is clear for us today. We are responsible for the words that God has left for us. Luke 6:46-49 is very plain and pointed. We have the responsibility to learn them, teach them, promote them, apply them, and defend them. When our will (whether or not it is as flagrant as these false teachers) clashes with the will of God, we have the responsibility to submit our will to God's will-- in every instance. Commitment is the basis of conversion and discipleship.

V.11 Woe to them! For they have gone the way of Cain, and for pay they have rushed headlong into the error of Balaam, and perished in the rebellion of Korah.

Jude begins this verse with a statement of misery that will soon come to pass on the false teachers when he states Woe to them! This statement is in the style of Jesus Christ and can be especially found in Matt 23:13*ff* in what has been popularly called The Seven Woes. But see also Revelation 8:13 and read Zephaniah during your lunch period next Tuesday.

Just a note here on the word 'Woe!' A good rule of thumb that will help you go far in your Bible reading and Christian walk. Anytime someone pronounces 'Woe!' upon someone or some group of folks in either the Old or the New Testament, you as the Bible reader ought to do two things almost reflexively. One, take note of what the recipient is being Woe'd for. Two, examine yourself and make sure that particular Woe'able item isn't in your life. Just a thought. Back to Jude.

Jude refers back to a trio of Old Testament folks and incidents to show the error of these men. These three incidents can be read in the Old Testament with little difficulty of understanding. The rebellion of Korah is found in Numbers chapter 16 and shows Korah's false accusations of Moses and Aaron in claiming that they set themselves above the Israelites.

He also complained that Moses failed to bring the nation into the promised land. We could stop there, but the greatest tragedy would be lost. If you are not familiar with the story of Korah, take the time to read it.

Who was Korah? A Levite, already set apart from the rest of the nation of Israel to be her priest. Korah was also a cousin of both Aaron and Moses. Happy? Not hardly. Though it doesn't specifically state so in the text, one can easily see the ego that Korah has--and it is bruised! At this writing, I am more than half a century old. All of my life, save a few years, has been spent in church buildings. When the doors flung open on Sunday mornings, Sunday nights, midweek and gospel meetings, our family was usually the first to fall in. What I'm saying is that I have seen my fair share of church squabbles. Add to that a dozen years of formal preaching and reading (between the lines) about church squabbles, splits and closures. It is always said about the split that it was for 'Biblical Reasons.' Yet, however, it is always primarily about personalities, egos and misguided leaders. What is going on where you work and worship? I pray all is well.

Look once again at Korah. He wasn't happy with just the assignment that God (not Moses) had given him. He pressed, cajoled, bamboozled or otherwise coaxed two hundred fifty respected elders to join him in his complaint (by, of course, tweaking *their* egos as well!). He basically said that he wanted to hear the final outcome straight from the horse's mouth! See where I'm headed with this? Nothing has changed. I tragically wonder what Korah was thinking at the very instant when the ground opened up and he headed south. Are you happy where you are in the local body? If not, how do you handle it? Hopefully, not in the same was as Korah.

In the error of Balaam found in Numbers chapter 31, we see his name as a symbol of materialism and avarice, though he started out pretty well in Numbers chapter 22. I'm sorry, the word avarice isn't something we use every day. How about this: good ol' fashioned greed, especially for money! Go back to Mark chapter 4 and see again what Jesus had to say about the deceitfulness of riches and the desire, or lust, for other things. He also said something in Matthew chapter 6 about trying to serve two masters--it simply can't be done.

Do we try it? Of course. In fact, our whole Christian walk may be taken up with attempting to make the final break between serving the two masters.

Greed isn't just a noun. It is, according to Scripture, idolatry. Idolatry is idol worship. Doesn't have to be a little carved monkey on the mantle or something out in the front yard with flowers and jewels all over it to be an idol. Still don't think so? Try Ephesians 4:5 and Colossians 3:5. Anything, no ANYTHING that places itself on the throne in place of God (Rich Young Ruler of Lk 18) is an idol. Balaam was overtaken with the thought of becoming rich. He did become rich, but only for a little while. When he died, they may have buried his riches with him, but wherever that place was, those riches are still there. He is not. No hearse ever pulled a U-Haul. Question: have you worked through the greed in your life? If not, why not?

The way of Cain may either be his attitude with his sacrifice, and therefore his attitude toward God, or the occasion of his murdering his brother Abel. One certainly led to another (I Jno 3:11*f*), so you pick. I suppose that Satan had a big hoop-dee-doo when Abel died. Satan managed to wipe out a significant percentage of the human race with that one murder. I'm sure that the seed promise of Genesis 3 was still ringing in Cain's ears when sin crouched at his door. Cain's attitudes and actions didn't work. Can't work. Won't work--but it still cost Cain his relationship with God. Jude doesn't want any more to follow.

We're still seeing mini-Cains in the church today. Don't get your way? Take your marbles elsewhere. Don't like a particular brother or sister? Go to the next church house. On your way, drop enough words (James 4) to ensure that the brother or sister will be a long time recovering. Allow me some time here on the church house shuffle.

At times it seems that the whole brotherhood is one big nomadic tribe--within a city! I've read the entire Bible through on several occasions and I cannot find one place where church hopping is sanctioned. We cite Paul and Barnabas fussing over John Mark in Acts 15:39 and use this as an example of how to conduct church. In reality, Luke is simply recording the events--and never once pronounces God's blessings on the split. It is my opinion that we need to spend more time and effort settling our differences when they arise (and they will, since we are human) and save the nomadic movements for extreme (real?) cases. Not the cases that we usually pin them on--just because our feelings are hurt and/or we don't get our little programmatic way.

Local congregations of the Lord's people are expedient. I currently live in El Paso. I live on the west side. I'm sure glad there is a church that meets a few minutes from my house. I don't want to drive for 45 minutes across the Franklin Mountains and across town to meet with the brethren. Local congregations are expedient. They *are not* a safe harbor for Cains. Back to Jude.

Jude is relating to the recipients of his epistle that the evil that these three Old Testament examples exhibited was working in the lives of the false teachers who were disrupting the church. Could it really be that these false teachers had a common ground with Cain, Balaam and Korah? Yes, as ugly as that prospect might seem. Jude also promises that their fate would be the same. No, the ground wasn't going to open up and swallow the false teachers. Their donkeys weren't going to talk and they weren't going to receive a physical mark on their person for all to see. But their *fate* would be the same: away from the Lord and His blessings forever (II Thess 1:9)! God, who is the author of time, is not affected by it. We are. We need to ever keep in mind that time does not water down God's view of His will, nor the consequences of breaking it.

That last statement is one that is easy to forget with the passing of time.

It is well worth pausing here and reflecting on the Old Testament, which takes up 76% of our Bible. There is (and I guess always will be) a thought in Christendom that states there is no need for the Old Testament whatsoever. Indeed, as one person so boldly put it to me once, one could rip the Old Testament from the Bible and throw it away and suffer no loss and be unchanged. Is that true? We still print New Testaments only by the double bucket load each year. The question arises as we examine this verse from Jude how one could know anything about Cain, Balaam or Korah were it not for the Old Testament? Well, I guess we could go to the internet. Boy, I'd hate to base my walk with Christ on internet info.

One Sunday morning I began an adult Bible class on an Old Testament book. One sister, who carried a New Testament only, complained after class that, "We are living in the New Testament (*sic*) and should be studying from it only." She gave me the added emphasis of folding her arms and adding a 'humph' at the end of her statement. I asked her (nicely!) what Jesus' point was in Matthew 21:42 and 22:29. I asked her to read Romans 15:4 and First Corinthians 10:6 and think about what Paul meant, again, nicely. The next Sunday she had a complete Bible. The Bible contains 66 entries, not 27. The Bible starts with "In the beginning," not "The book of the generation of Jesus Christ." We've got to include the Old Testament heeds and deeds.

Another thought. A church was meeting in a school not too far from my house. The school had let them meet there while they raised enough money for a church building. I had regular occasions to pass by on Sunday mornings as folks scurried from their cars to their seats. I watched as folks came in and out of the school building (two services) and very few were carrying Bibles. I've witnessed this phenomena in other places, even where I ministered. As far as I know, the only place that God's will for mankind can be found is in-between Genesis and Maps.

God has spoken concerning His "Old Testament" and given us today the purpose behind its preservation. It may be time well spent to review passages such as First Corinthians 10:1-12 and Romans 15:4 and the message will ring loud and clear: do not do as the ancients did when they forsook God. Conversely, we are to emulate those upon whom God has given His stamp of approval through their faithful lives and devotion to Him. That is the message of Hebrews chapter 11. Jude uses these Old Testament examples at the very apex of his warnings. Without these particular stories preserved (as they certainly were during Jude's time), one would be hard pressed today to grasp any true, life changing meaning from the references to them.

V.12 These men are those who are hidden reefs in your love feasts when they feast with you without fear, caring for themselves; clouds without water, carried along by winds; autumn trees without fruit, doubly dead, uprooted;

Jude now refers to these men as hidden reefs, from the Greek *spilas*. This noun only occurs once in the Bible, but has been translated in many different ways can be evidenced by the following list of popular translations:

KJV/TEV	"spots"	ASV	"hidden rocks"
NIV/RSV	"blemishes"	NASB	"hidden reefs"
Message	"warts"	CEV	"filthy minded"

The word *spilas* actually is to be translated to mean a craggy rock or reef over which the sea dashes; or a rock or reef hidden by the water. The translators who were responsible for using the words *spot* or *blemish* perhaps tried to make this passage equivalent to Second Peter 2:13, where the Greek *spilos* is used and there should rightly be translated *spots*. Sorry, I'm a stickler for that kind of stuff. One letter change can make a difference: *spilas/spilos*, rum/run, stomp/stump, lice/lick, you get my drift. You can run for rum, lick lice and stomp on a stump, but that's about all they have in common.

When reading this verse, one generates the idea that the Christians were seeing, and expecting, smooth sailing ahead and not realizing that they were sailing into a shipwreck situation with these men. These hidden reefs were long since past the point of being mere spots but were now elements of danger and wreck to the church. This amplifies the danger of wayward leaders. People *want* to line up under leaders. They *want* leaders to lead.

Looking back over the years I filled pulpits in local congregations, I well remember the beginning of each work. Expectation of great things filled the church. As with no other time, people were willing to make sacrifices of time and money to advance the church's programs.

They were ready for something new and exciting to

happen. Looking back, how dangerous is that? Pretty dangerous if the leader is off course. And Jude says that those in his time were hidden. Now, how dangerous is that!? We've all hit the potholes while driving along a dark road. I would say a country road, but I've driven downtown Columbus, Ohio. If we were expecting it, we would have slowed way down. I remember a man driving in West Texas around the town of Kermit. He drove his truck into a sinkhole which swallowed his car. Had he known it was there, he would have taken a different route. One morning while fishing on the banks of the James River in Virginia, I watched a man, running full throttle, standing up in his boat. He hit a sandbar. Good thing he knew how to swim. Didn't find most of his equipment. So it is with leaders who lead away. If a church had known...

Caring for themselves is literally *feeding themselves*. The word *feeding* is from the Greek *poimaino*, a word that means to *feed* or *tend a flock*. A *poimen* is a shepherd, by which we have elsewhere in the Scriptures translated pastor or shepherd. Jude may be metaphorically speaking, or he may be referencing the local leadership, thereby identifying them as the false teachers. While this 'metaphor identification' is not for certain and is without textual proof, it is ever true that, "As the leadership goes, so goes the church." The admonition to Timothy concerning elders may take on a fresh sense of urgency as one reads First Timothy 5:17-25. Read the First Timothy section critically. Start by reading First Timothy 5:22-24:

Do not lay hands upon anyone too hastily and thus share responsibility for the sins of others; keep yourself free from sin. No longer drink water exclusively, but use a little wine for the sake of your stomach and your frequent ailments. The sins of some men are quite evident, going before them to judgment; for others, their sins follow after.

Then read it again, taking out the parenthetical statement about Timothy's health found in verse 23:

Do not lay hands upon anyone too hastily and thus share responsibility for the sins of others; keep yourself free from sin. The sins of some men are quite evident, going before them to judgment; for others, their sins follow after.

The point? Paul was still talking about church leaders--shepherds--when he was reminded of Timothy's health problems. As far as I know, first century parchments and scrolls didn't all come with cut and paste options. Some folks' sins aren't as easily discerned up front. It is only after they are placed in a 'we will follow you' category that the seeds of devastation are planted, grow and do their work in a local congregation. My personal feelings on the subject? Jude is talking about the leaders of the local or regional church. Again, scary thought.

In the days prior to the throw-a-switch irrigation, the farmers among the first century church knew well of clouds without water. When rain is needed, one looks expectantly to the clouds. Likewise, Christians look expectantly to the teachers who have a high degree of responsibility (and, therefore, accountability) toward their brothers and sisters. This responsibility of teachers is seen in the opening of the third chapter of James when he writes to the irresponsible recipients of that letter, "Let not many of <u>you</u> become teachers."

The church today spends the majority of its funds on physical plants followed by its paid staff which includes the minister only in smaller families to a rather large staff of secretaries and several ministers in the bigger churches. With the threat of waterless clouds always looming on the horizon and the great responsibility resting on their shoulders, isn't it time that the church of today should look to training Bible teachers to 'be all that they can be?' Yes, I'm talking about the good Brothers and Sisters who teach the three year olds and the Youth Groups!

The last metaphor is of the autumn trees without fruit. It not only bears no fruit, but is dead. It is not only dead but doubly so. It is not only doubly dead, but has been uprooted-- a term which may be referencing the judgment upon the false teachers. One cannot read this metaphor without being reminded of the parable of the fig tree found in Luke chapter 13 where Jesus says of the barren tree, "Cut it down! Why does it even use up the ground?" Now *that's* a sad commentary on anyone: so un-useful that they are accused of just taking up space. Doubly so on church leaders. My Dad told me once that no one is totally useless--you can always use them as a doorstop. A doorstop. Wow, not much there.

A little more on church leader training. While ministering for a medium sized congregation, I approached the elders about appropriating funds to train the elders and deacons directly. I was looking for about $100-150 per head, 5 or 6 leaders in all. The answer was no.

Within a couple of months, we appropriated nearly $1200 to spruce up the building on a workday. I'm all for keeping up a building. No one wants to sit in a stinky ramshackle hut with little church mice and roaches running hither and yon. However, I believe we should be for sprucing up all of our leaders, equipping them for the awesome work of leading souls to Christ and ultimately to Heaven. Spiffy church building full of corpses. Wow, not much there.

V.13 wild waves of the sea, casting up their own shame like foam; wandering stars, for whom the black darkness has been reserved forever.

Jude applies a metaphor to the false teachers as being like the wild waves of the sea. And just as the waves are indeed uncontrollable by mankind, so it might seem of these disrupters. When foam is cast up on the beach, it is deposited there for all to see. Beach foam usually stinks, too, full of decaying fish bits and trash. Such is the shame of those Jude is addressing. He also applies the metaphor of their being wandering stars. Jude may be referring to what is commonly known as shooting stars. They burn brightly for a time, but only because they are burning out. After a brief brightness they are to shine no more and are committed to the black darkness as they disappear from our sight.

We don't know much about Hell, therefore, we will continue to debate, fuss, write and speak about it till the end of time. Jude calls it a black darkness. Jesus called it a continuously burning fire as He compared it to the trash pits of Jerusalem that continuously burned. Paul said that those not in Heaven would be shut out from the presence of the Lord, forever.

The reason we debate and fuss is because all descriptions of Hell (and Heaven for that matter) are described to us in figures of speech. Mankind can, however, understand some basic principles of these two eternal destinations: Heaven is a good and desirable place while Hell is just the opposite. Let's leave it at that and strive for the one place while avoiding the other.

What is sad about this black darkness for these disrupters is that it came with a reservation. In our society today a reservation is a good thing. Did you make a reservation? Good, you don't have to wait forty-five minutes at the seafood joint on a Friday night. Did you make a reservation? Good, you can get your hair all done up on a Saturday afternoon before that hot date. But a reservation for Hell?! THAT can be avoided by simply making a reservation for Heaven.

V.14 And about these also Enoch, the seventh from Adam, prophesied, saying, "Behold, the Lord came with many thousands of His holy ones,

Little is written about the Old Testament character Enoch. Outside of Jude he is only mentioned in the genealogies of Genesis chapter 5, Luke chapter 3, and is mentioned by Luke in Hebrews 11:5 in regards to his faith. Much is known, however, about Enoch by what was written about him. A summary of his character is simply stated in Genesis 5:24 where we find that "Enoch walked with God." If that is on one's tombstone, it would be enough.

Also, much can be learned from the statement that Enoch was the seventh from Adam, through the line of Seth. Now, at this point I refuse to talk about the creation, the age of the earth, the age of man, chimps, the H.M.S. *Beagle* or L.S.B & Mary Leakey--or any australopithecines that may or may not have been running around. What I do want to mention here is parents teaching their children.

The lesson is this: Seth taught his kids about God. They taught their kids about God, who in turn taught their kids about God, and finally Jared taught his kid, Enoch, about God.

Contrast that with Cain who probably dropped the ball and we got folks in the linage of Cain like Lamech who bragged that he was the biggest, baddest dude on the Mesopotamian block, and proved it by killing a kid who hit him. Wow, that's one tough hombre, wouldn't you say? But we get the lesson. If Christian parents don't teach their kids about God, then the kids will soon be introduced to a world without God.

Enoch had to have been speaking of a time future to him when the Lord would come with His angels in judgment upon the earth. Neither the universal flood nor the end of time had arrived by the time of his translation to the home office, so each would be a possible candidate. Since Enoch was taken by God quite a number of years before the flood, this is probably a reference to that incident. If speaking in the future of the end of time and subsequent judgment of mankind, Enoch is in harmony with Paul's teaching in Second Thessalonians 1:6-10.

Or, he was speaking of both. To ascribe Enoch's prophecy to both the flood and the end of time would pose no problem and would certainly not be the only dual prophecy in the Bible. For example in Isaiah: a child born of a virgin...

Either way the message is clear: God warns first, but because He is a just God judgment is inevitable for the unrepentant. God will only allow something or someone that is attacking His church to exist for only so long. In fact, that is the underlying message found in the book of Revelation. That alone should bring hope to the Christian.

V.15 to execute judgment upon all, and to convict all the ungodly of all their ungodly deeds which they have done in an ungodly way, and of all the harsh things which ungodly sinners have spoken against Him.

Jude continues the prophecy of Enoch which started in verse 14. The most prominent word in this verse is the word ungodly occurring four times. The word ungodly is the Greek word *asebes* and describes a lack of reverence toward God, or impiety. When God comes to execute judgment upon all, He will convict all those whose deeds and speech lack reverence toward Him. Again, we are reminded of the parallel teachings of Jesus as He said:

That which proceeds out of the man, that is what defiles the man. For from within, out of the heart of men, proceed the evil thoughts and fornication, thefts, murders, adulteries, deeds of coveting and wickedness, as well as deceit, sensuality, envy, slander, pride, and foolishness. All these evil things proceed from within and defile the man. Mk 7:20-23

See also Matthew 12:36 and note that it means what it says. See also Second Corinthians 5:10 and note that it means what it says, also. It would be expedient here to note again the theme of the letter: *God has, and will always condemn evil doers*.

Because of the swift and harsh tone of the writer there is little doubt that he had in mind the men who were dividing and disrupting the recipient church, as is clearly seen in the opening phrase of the preceding verse. We can only conclude that the same fate follows those unrepentant disrupters of the Lord's church today, for God has not placed a time limit on it.

V.16 These are grumblers, finding fault, following after their own lusts; they speak arrogantly, flattering people for the sake of gain saying an advantage.

Jude now describes the ungodly of the recipient church by calling them grumblers, from the Greek *gongudzo*. This word is onomatopoeic, wherein the significance of the word is represented by the sound in the original language. I like this word. An easier word that is onomatopoeic is the word *buzz*. It is spelled like it sounds. This word *gongudzo* may have originated from the word for sea shell, and is used to describe the sound one hears when a shell is placed up to the ear. It is also used for the cooing of doves. I've got doves here where I live. I can't understand a word they are cooing.

As used in the New Testament, *gongudzo* in its noun form only appears in Jude, though the verb form is all over the place. It fits those who grumble, mutter, or speak privately and in a low voice. In general, it is used to describe one who is complaining. Because such murmurings are usually complaints, it speaks of discontent

Grumbling, though it would seem commonplace in some

churches today, is considered to be a sin by New Testament teachings. In John 6:41 & 43 we see Jesus telling the Jews not to grumble or complain. Later, in verse 6, Jesus had to deal with murmuring disciples. In First Corinthians 10:10 Paul used the Israelites who grumbled against God after the exodus as an example--they were destroyed. In Philippians 2:14*ff* we are given the directive not to grumble, so that we can prove ourselves blameless, innocent, and above reproach. The grumblers are further described as finding fault, which means they found dissatisfaction with all who were around them. That which leads them to be fault finders and grumblers is found in the fact that they were following after their own lusts.

One who behaves in this way, at the expense of following God, will lead the unhappy life attested to these men. The meaning of the phrase they speak arrogantly may best be shown by the RSV translation that states, "they are loud-mouthed boasters." Peterson in *The Message* calls them *grumpers and bellyachers!* The reason for their behavior is in order to flatter people around them for the sake of gaining an advantage. This type of advantage is false and, as with all sin, is short lived in any advantage it might bring a person.

I'm never sure of the advantage, however. The question will ever be, "What does a person hope to gain by putting a frown on his or her face, looking past any good that might be out there and dwelling on all of the grump and gruff?" What stone do we expect to turn over with our complaining? What soul do we possibly hope to sway in a positive way by behaving negatively? In reality, the person who grumbles will be like the proverbial painter who came ever so close to finishing the task at hand, only to find he had painted himself into a corner and now is subject to the paint--he must wait until it dries!

One Sunday morning I was standing at the back of the foyer after an exceptionally hard hitting sermon, though the subject is now lost to me. It was one of those sermons that I had sweated over for several weeks. Not an axe to grind or the launching of a new program (neither of which, I believe, have any place in the pulpit), but the rubber-meets-the-road, take a look at your spiritual life type of sermon. One could see why a preacher would be nervous. The lesson was delivered and was accepted. Brothers and sisters began to shake my hand. They didn't give the usual, "Nice sermon, Preach" or "Good job" but made specific comments on how that sermon really made them take inventory. Because I'm human, I began to feel pretty good about my accomplishments that morning. Wave after wave of positive comments poured in. Next in line was a little blue haired sister who obviously wanted to say something to me.

"I got here this morning and there wasn't any toilet paper in the stall. Why can't you make sure that there is toilet paper in the women's stalls before you open up? I had to get someone to go get some. You're in charge here and you could do better!" Now you see why I can't remember what the sermon was about.

Yes, it *is* important to have toilet paper--especially at critical times. Yes, this sister did knock me down a notch in my exponentially building ego that morning. But you see, she didn't, *couldn't*, share in the moment with everyone else that morning for grumping about the toilet paper.

We don't get our way so we whine. We want something to change so we grump. We want someone different so we criticize. We want a new situation so we denounce. We want a different pace so we fuss.

Though uninspired, at times we ought to heed the warning that we've all heard: "If you can't say anything nice, don't say anything at all." Uninspired, but true. Go rent Walt Disney's *Bambi*. I think Flower said it. Maybe Thumper.

Pick any arena you like: religious, political, business, social clubs, you name it--if you are Gretta Grump or Freddie Frump, folks will soon avoid you. In the first arena, religious, you have now become ineffective. Worse than that, you have now switched sides and are batting for the other team.

Yes, you are now batting for the other team. Doesn't matter what uniform you happen to be wearing.

Christians Will Escape the Wrath of God, verses 17-25

I didn't write Jude. Jude did. I can see the reasons why he wrote the things he did and in the order that he wrote them. There were some things--no, some folks--who had wormed their way into leadership spots and were tearing the church apart from the inside out. That had to stop. Hopefully, his words started that stopping motion.

But now there is the fallout. The aftermath. The wounded and dying disciples of Christ that were the casualties of the carnage. As we saw in the beginning of this book, soldiers of Christ never leave their wounded on the battlefield. Never. This final section is the field manual for clearing the field of those wounded disciples.

V.17 But you, beloved, ought to remember the words that were spoken beforehand by the apostles of our Lord Jesus Christ

Jude now takes the beloved reader back to the words that were spoken beforehand by the apostles. He recognized that this is what the faith of the Christian is built upon. Jesus spoke of the perpetual authority of the words of the apostles in John 17:20*f.* Paul recognized this foundation of faith that the apostles laid in Ephesians 2:20, with Christ being the corner stone (I Cor 3:11). If Jude had been numbered with the apostles, he more likely than not would have included himself with them. I guess he would have. I would have, wouldn't you?

Some scholars believe that this statement is proof that all of the apostles had died by this time. By mentioning the fact that the words were spoken of in the past is not conclusive evidence that the apostles are in the past also. One must remember that in verse 3, Jude speaks of the faith having been once for all delivered to the saints. Perhaps some were still alive, but at this point no new revelation was being given to the church. Worth thinking about if nothing else. I believe at times we attempt to stretch the apostles' and inspired writers' ages almost to the unimaginable breaking point. We have some really old patriarchs early on in Genesis, but by Jesus' day folks didn't live even as long as we do now, by a long shot. Verse 17 is an opening statement to remind the church of a prophecy that was pronounced by the apostles and will be seen in the next verse.

Another item to note in this verse is the phrase, "But you, beloved..." It will surface again in a few verses. God has always given the solution along with the problem. Note how many times in the Old and New Testament that writers have listed *Thou Shall Nots*. Each time, the *However, Thou Shalls* are close behind. Isn't that a benevolent God? He never leaves us hanging, wondering what *to do* now that we have been told what *not* to do. The same is true in Jude--there are some that are tearing the church right off of her very foundation of Jesus and the Apostle's teachings!

What can the regular, God-fearing disciples do? In verse 17, the answer is clear--go back to your roots in the biblical teachings of the Apostles! What advice for the child of God today. Get back into the Bible. Stop making man the primary source of our spiritual feeding. Stop making the Sunday sermon our only trip to the feed bag. What an army God would have upon the face of the earth, if we would just heed Jude's teaching--But you, beloved...

When disciples of Christ rely solely on one man delivering their only feeding for 30 minutes on Sunday morning, their understanding of the Word becomes shallower and shallower until finally it dries leaving behind sun baked mud cracks. When the family of God in a local church is well versed in the Scriptures, it becomes nearly impossible for false and skewed teachings to gain that toe hold that is needed for infection. And pray. Pray like your spiritual life depended on it.

It does.

V.18 that they were saying to you, "In the last time there shall be mockers, following after their own ungodly lusts."

In this verse we are given the prophecy of the apostles. It would be unreasonable to think that the whole prophecy consisted of these words, but rather this is simply the part of the prophecy that Jude wished to remind the church of at this time. In the last time should be taken to mean the Christian dispensation. There will not be another dispensation after this time that we live in today. I repeat...there will not be another dispensation after this time that we live in today. What greater dispensation than this one, where we enjoy salvation from our sins because of a sacrifice on a cross one Friday long ago, can there possibly be? All things have been delivered. We await Christ's return.

Neither are we to think that anytime we come across mockers, following after their own ungodly lusts, we are to think that the Lord's coming is at hand, although we should live our lives in expectation of the glorious event. The apostle Paul taught in the first Thessalonian letter that the day of the Lord would come as a thief in the night (5:2), just as the Lord had taught during His earthly ministry (Mt 24:42*ff*). Jude simply states that these false teachers are mockers and does not preserve the content of their mockery for us today. We may gain some insight from the parallel passage found in Second Peter 3:3*f* where the apostle Peter says that they will be asking, "Where is the promise of (Christ's) coming?" Whatever the ungodly were mocking, their actions were plain--they were following after their own ungodly lusts.

Some see the reference in this verse to 'saying' rather than 'writing' (and in verse 17) would denote that Jude was writing to the church in Jerusalem. This would be about the only place that a plurality of apostles would have been all in one place teaching the church. This is certainly not without merit, but don't allow the cleaving of rabbits to distract from the message of Jude. Leave the hare splitting to the scholars. Absorb the message.

We're used to mockers that are outside of the church. I remember in Oregon one Saturday while our teens were hanging a banner across the front of the church building in preparation for a Vacation Bible School. Other teens were walking by and saying, "Hey, give it up. God is dead. Go home and enjoy your Saturday!" We don't like it, but we're used to it. But how about mockers *inside* the church? Again, almost unimaginable. Until we realize the implications of the next verse:

V.19 These are the ones who cause divisions, worldly-minded, devoid of the Spirit.

At this point in the letter, Jude now becomes more direct and specific in pointing out the problems in the church and the causes of them. It is as if he is pointing a finger at the false teachers and stating that these are the ones who cause divisions in the church. It is only when these false teachers find listening ears that their false doctrines and practices will (or even can) be spread. The same is true today, so think about it the next time someone tries to bend your ear with junk. Not junk from the radio or television. Not junk from the world's billboards, radio and television programs or backroom conversations. Junk in the church foyer, church hallway, fellowship room-- or even worse, from the pulpit or lecture room. The apostle Paul described divisions and factions as quarrels in First Corinthians 1:11, and James used the word translated *wars* in James 4:1.

Because these divisive people were worldly-minded, they had lost contact with God. One cannot have his mind on the world and on God at the same time. Jesus taught that no man can serve two masters (Mt 6:24) even though we sometimes try ever so hard, and we are commanded to set our minds on the things above, not on earthly things (Col 3:2). As a result of the actions of the worldly-minded, they are now devoid of the (Holy) Spirit. For us today, we can see that it is the same type of people who cause divisions in the house of God. Think back on any division in the church that you have experienced or been aware of, and you will find, not a battle over right and wrong, good and evil, but a battle of personalities (Betcha a dollar to a donut...betcha, betcha, betcha!). Personalities which have as their goal such items as their own way, an object (such as a program or a new building), or just to win. Divisive preachers, pastors, bishops, priests, elders, teachers, and others may proclaim loudly that they are doing God's work, but when the end result is division, one must wonder...and ultimately is left with God's judgment through Scripture.

"Well, that's just the way that she is," is a phrase I heard concerning a woman when her disruptive and abusive actions were talked about in a leaders' meeting one evening. A second sister had made a set of curtains in one of the church rooms to replace a set that had long years ago faded and were in the last stages of sun baked deterioration. The new seamstress had been through quite an ordeal in her personal life that had left her devastated and withdrawn for many months. Her very godly, very evangelistic--and very young--husband had been killed while he stopped to assist someone on the side of the road. She was left a young widowed mother. The curtains were her way of 'getting back into the swing of things' and one step closer to body life. The other sister, whose actions we were now discussing, happened by the church building midweek and noticed the new curtains. The curtains were ripped from their rods and the next thing I knew, they were tossed into my office floor as the angry woman wondered just who had the gall to take down *her* curtains that she had made (a hundred years prior, I might add)! I explained that our widowed sister, who had been through quite a life and had been withdrawn, made those and, "Isn't it wonderful that she did that for us?"

"No!" was the shouted reply. "You can just tell her that her curtains are in the trash, and where are *my* curtains that I made?"

The "Well, that's just the way that she is," phrase came from an elder. As one would expect, a battle raged over the next couple of months. When the battle was finally over, the sister who made the new curtains was gone, along with her children. The woman who tore down the curtains was pleased with herself. The church was divided. It was called a biblical matter. It was not. It was people who were worldly-minded, devoid of the Spirit.

V.20 But you, beloved, building yourselves up on your most holy faith; praying in the Holy Spirit;

Jude, now and throughout the remainder of the epistle, turns his attention away from the divisive people to those who have not abandoned the faith. There is a lesson to be learned from the way Jude addressed the problem as a whole. It is to no advantage to write about the problem if there is to be no discussion as to the answer to that problem. Too often this is lacking in our teaching today: too much information and not enough application. Too much whining and not enough solution. As disciples of Christ we must not only *learn* God's word but we must learn *what to do* with His word in relationship to our lives and the lives of those around us. I rather think that Jesus had this in mind when He spoke what we've come to know as the Great Commission:

And Jesus came up and spoke to them, saying, "All authority has been given to Me in heaven and on earth. Go therefore and make disciples of all the nations, baptizing them in the name of the Father and the Son and the Holy Spirit, teaching them to observe all that I commanded you; and lo, I am with you always, even to the end of the age." Matt 28:18-20

Notice that Jesus didn't say that we should be taught all that He commanded, but that we should learn to observe all that He commanded. Big difference. The former is easy. The latter takes a lifetime.

The beginning place in the correcting of the problems of the church is with the individuals themselves before they do battle with the false teachers. We are told to put on the whole armor of God in Ephesians. In this passage Paul lists many defensive items metaphorically, and one offensive one--the sword of the Spirit, which is the word of God. Jude means no less when he tells these recipients to build themselves up in their most holy faith. They cannot contend earnestly for that which they cannot grasp or understand. One cannot go into battle dressed in sandals and Bermuda shorts. Well, you could, but you would be the first to fall.

Too many have fallen.

They are not to do battle by themselves, but are to have the avenue of prayer and utilize it. Not in some mystical, invocational way, but in a way that is full of faith, knowing and believing that God hears and answers prayers, knowing and believing that God understands our hearts even when we don't know how or what to ask for. This type of prayer would be praying in the Holy Spirit. Praying in the Holy Spirit is *not* sounding like a football fanatic at a home game when the home boys suddenly score a big fat touchdown. Neither is it looking or sounding like one just stepped barefoot into a sticker patch. Praying in the Holy Spirit is outlined in Scripture. We don't need to make something up to accompany it. After speaking of the armor of God in Ephesians chapter 6, the apostle Paul commands that at all times 'pray in the Spirit.' For the evidence that the Spirit does indeed assist the believer in prayer read Romans 8:26 and First Corinthians 14:15. The Spirit aids us when we are unable to word our prayers and petitions. I'm glad. How about you?

Again, Jude leaves the rank and file disciple with what to do when seemingly overwhelmed with the bad news of those attempting to divide the church: build yourselves through prayer. We must ask, "How often do I really practice that type of prayer in my life when things are *going right*, let alone *wrong?*" I truly believe, that if I'm asked by anyone, anywhere, "What is wrong with my church? How can we improve? Why aren't we moving?" that I can confidently answer, without ever stepping into a building or attending a worship, "You don't pray enough" and in most instances, be right on target! When we pray, we abandon self and rely on God. Add to that Bible reading and one has a complete circle of communication with God--He talks, we listen; we talk, He listens. Neat, huh? Works in a marriage, too.

What is the result of much and fervent prayer? Verse 21, so read on.

V.21 keep yourselves in the love of God, waiting anxiously for the mercy of our Lord Jesus Christ to eternal life.

The opening phrase of this verse, keep yourselves in the love of God, seems to be a summation of the preceding verse. One can accomplish much if he remains in the love of God. The phrase denotes more by the word keep. Although man can do nothing to earn his salvation, man can do much in the way of retaining that saving relationship with Jesus. Works, though they have no part in salvation, have much to do with the life of the Christian in their walk. We were created for good works and should walk in them (Eph 2:10). Some today shrug off all talk of works as a pendulum swing to legalism. Our daily walk is manifested by our works of faith (I Jno 1:7) and even Jesus said His followers would know a little something about their fellow man by the life that each one leads (Mt 7:16). That we cannot earn our salvation is evident in the next phrase, waiting anxiously for the mercy of eternal life with Christ. Mercy, defined, is simply when we don't receive that which we deserve, as opposed to grace, when we receive that which we don't deserve.

Again, to keep yourselves in the love of God is given to us as *our* action. There is nothing as toothless as the teaching that we cannot earn our salvation (true!), so *therefore* (here comes the rationalized untruth) we need to just praise God and generally do nothing that would smack of us trying to do anything that would remotely seem like we are trying to aid God in retaining… blah, blah, blab! It just isn't that way in our Christian walk. God saves, we respond. We respond with a life that if full of fruit, earnestly seeking others who will listen to the gospel, contending earnestly for the faith, and waiting anxiously for the mercy of eternal life with Christ.

I'm well aware of the promise that Jesus gives His followers recorded in John 10. We're in the Father's hand and no one is able to snatch us out. Who tries? Satan tries, but it can't be done. He tries through empty promises from the world. He tries through damaging, yet well-meaning people. He tries, and keeps on trying. However, there is nothing in that promise--as miraculous and wonderful as it is, that precludes Satan standing off in the distance coaxing and coaching us off the Master's hand. He accomplishes this well by ramming the idea down the throats of our theology that we simply don't need to do anything, just go on like nothing has changed! Jude certainly had a different idea.

Jude describes the Master by way of a three-fold appellation: our Lord Jesus Christ. By this name, Jude has described Him as the historical incarnate God, Jesus, who is both Lord and Christ. This is the very way that Peter finished his first sermon on the day of Pentecost declaring that it was God who made Jesus both Lord and Christ.

In respect to Peter's Pentecostal sermon, we often rush to verse 37 and 38 to reach a conclusion: repentance and immersion for forgiveness. True, but isn't it time we study what Peter said to those folks to cause them to ask, "What must I do?" Well worth reading the entire sermon, dissecting it and seeing just what caused 3,000 men (probably not counting the ladies, who traditionally make up the majority of any church body) to repent and be immersed for the forgiveness of their sins.

V.22 And have mercy on some, who are doubting;

This verse, though short, has much in the way of a directive on how to deal with some who are doubting. Jude does not say to deal harshly with those who are in error through honest doubt, but rather to deal with them in the same manner that the Lord has with all that He would save. Mercy is a trait that each disciple is to carry in life, and continue to mature it as a life trait. To know that it is not an option for each person, one only needs to read Matthew 5:7. James picked up on this in 2:13. Our Lord is a merciful Lord and we are to deal with each other just as the Lord has dealt with us. This can be seen in commandments such as the one found in Ephesians 4:32 and the counter verse seen in Colossians 3:13. Grace, mercy, and forgiveness are so closely interconnected that they are not easily dissected from each other. In fact, the gesture of forgiveness through the avenue of grace may well define a merciful person.

To see how Jesus deals with sinners compared with how we often deal with each other in religious matters (and just plain everyday life), study the parable of the two insolvent debtors in Matthew 18:23-35. Another name for this parable might well be the 'Parable of the Brain Damaged Servant' would it not offend us in our conviction. To further study how we are to deal with weak brothers, study Second Timothy 2:24-26 and, of course, Romans chapters 14 & 15. We usually speak in terms of 'Romans 14' in dealing with weak brethren. To be sure, the meat of the matter is in that chapter. But don't ever, ever leave out 15:1-7 in that study. That's where the conclusion is. That's where the hard part is.

I well remember, during my tenure in a local work, the brother that would sporadically attend the church leaders' meetings when there was a problem. To be sure, the problem was oftentimes fabricated between this brother's ears, but his answer to everything and everyone was, "Give them time to repent (which was about 30 seconds in his mind) and then ask them to leave!" No comment needed here!

Sorry, comment here. Jesus said something about logs and splinters when it comes to dealing with other people. How funny, yet ridiculous it must have seemed to those sitting around listening to the Master Story Teller speak of someone having a log in his eye trying to nit-pick another brother. Do note, however, before you go on to the end of the letter, just how many times Jude uses the word mercy and in what context. We are to have mercy on others if we are to receive the mercy that he prayed for in verse 2. Again the words of Jesus ring out again to us: we will be shown mercy if we show mercy (Matt 9:13, Lk 10, Jas 2:13). Incidentally, the converse is true, also.

V.23 save others, snatching them out of the fire; and on some have mercy with fear, hating even the garment polluted by the flesh.

The thought on how to deal with the weak is continued with verse 23 with the command to save others. The ones to be saved were on the brink of destruction as indicated by the phrase, snatching them out of the fire. The verb *to snatch* is the Greek *harpadzo*. This verb describes the act of seizing hastily by an overpowering, overwhelming force. It was used contemporarily to describe the act of robbery. The Septuagint (Greek rendering of the Old Testament, *ca* 270 B.C.), or LXX, contains this word in Zechariah 3:2 and Amos 4:11 to show God's action of pulling the nation of Israel out of the world to be His people. It is also used to describe the action of the Holy Spirit upon Philip in Acts 8:39, and upon Paul in Second Corinthians 12:2, 4 when he was caught up into Paradise.

In a roundabout way (Greek to Latin to Old French to Old English to our English) we get our word *harpoon*. Now that word will stick! If one reads Ezekiel (long about chapter 34...)

we see where the shepherds of Israel were to go bring back the wandering sheep. Not so they could peel 'em and eat 'em, but to return them to the fold. Binding up the lame...not in a Seattle wrap for lunch, but to restore them to the fold.

In Jude this word conveys the idea of force suddenly exercised upon a lost or straying person. It illustrates well for us how that person is swiftly, marvelously and permanently moved from one place to another--from a state of damnation to that of salvation. And still for others have mercy with fear. The attitude that they were to exhibit was discussed in the preceding verse. There was a warning added to this phrase, and that was that while showing mercy, they were to have fear, lest those giving the warning fall prey to the same sin that held those they were to help save from the fire. They were to hate even the garment polluted by the flesh, or to hate the ways of the flesh. The way that disciples are to view sinners is the same way that God views: hate the sin, but love the sinner.

Let's talk about snatching. We have lost the art of snatching. Jude wants us to snatch, we want to hem haw.

More than a long time ago I began preaching for a little church in West Texas. As with most new preachers, I began to inquire about those in town who, in some form or another, had been affiliated with the body of Christ but now were not. One couple was put before me as having been on fire for the Lord for many years, but suddenly just grew cold, withdrew and stopped attending the worship (I hate the phrase *stopped going to church*). I asked what measures the church had taken to bring them back. The church sent a card as best as anyone could remember. I gathered up a fellow disciple, we went and rang the doorbell. Both hubby and wife had seen us coming up the walk and both answered the door.

After introducing myself and asking if they had a little block of time to talk, I asked how their faith in God was (poor), how they saw their state with God (lost) and what we could do to assist them to get back on track with God (we talked for an hour), all with a cheerful, nice, non-condemning tone of voice. Upon leaving, the companion I had with me verbalized that I had been too forward and maybe a bit too pointed in my opening statement. I asked him if we should have spent our time with, "How's the weather, and how 'bout them

Cowboys?" "Well, yes!" was his reply, "We don't want to scare them off!"

What?! Is snatching not politically correct? No? Then it's biblically correct. The church is not *PC*, the church is *JC!* Besides, how could we have possibly scared these folks off? The next Sunday, the husband was back in the fold. A few months later the wife joined him after several years of both needing to be out of the fire.

The church today is in the soul snatching business. Nothing has changed. We get sidetracked by the entertainment in worship business, the busy business, the pacification through programs business and the building up of self-esteem business. The Bible knows the soul snatching business. Merciful snatching.

V.24 Now to Him who is able to keep you from stumbling, and to make you stand in the presence of His glory blameless with great joy,

In this verse Jude begins his doxology of the epistle. We must look ahead to the last verse to ascertain that the pronoun Him is in reference to God. Jude relates that God will be able to do two things for the Christian who walks in the light. He will be able to keep us from stumbling, and cause us to stand in the presence of His glory. All men, saved or not, will one day stand in the presence of the Almighty God (II Cor 5:10), but there is an adjective after the second phrase to describe how the Christian is to stand before God, and that is blameless. The one blaming, or accusing the child of God is Satan (Rev 12:10, but see also the first few verses of Zech 3), but to no avail when one walks in the light. The descriptive phrase with great joy is the only natural way to describe one who stands before God blameless.

This promise from the inspired writer should cause the Christian to seek to restore brothers who have fallen prey to false teachers (II Tim 2:26), such as were described in this epistle. Too many have left, walked out of both the church building and the church. Too many times we have allowed this to happen simply because we thought it more harmful to possibly hurt their feelings rather than allow them to walk--limp--into Hell. Couple this with empty, false or otherwise damaging preaching and teaching and we have the perfect ingredients for Satan's breeding ground. Make no mistake, Satan will be there. Wounded are ever so much easier to kill than vibrant, fighting Christian soldiers.

V.25 to the only God our Savior, through Jesus Christ our Lord, be glory, majesty, dominion and authority, before all time and now and forever. Amen.

Jude concludes his doxology by addressing the true nature of Deity, the only God our Savior, and relates that the Godhead works in the salvation process of man only through Jesus Christ our Lord. This is the plan that God has set forth for man, and that is through Jesus Christ our Lord. Jesus stated plainly in John 14:6 that it was through himself that salvation would come to man. I know, I know, there is someone reading this that would ask of me, "So, you think that there is only one God and He speaks through Jesus the Christ?"

Yep.

Jude believed that there is only one God and the only way to Him was through Jesus Christ. Jesus thought the same thing that God did and told us so in John 14:6. Peter thought this in Acts chapter 2 and Paul used this as a recurring theme in his letters to various churches and individuals. Jude ends his letter with One God, One Savior, One Way. If anything is creeping into the church today under the banners of toleration and unity through diversity, it is the idea of multiple roads to utopia and a plurality of Higher Powers out there somewhere. Is Jude for today? By now, I hope you are convinced!

Jude then praises God with the four-fold praise of glory, majesty, dominion and authority. Glory refers to the radiance of God (Lk 2:9) and is a term ascribed to Christ (Heb. 1:3). The majesty of God is His royalty (Heb 1:3; 8:1). His dominion is His rule (Ps 72:8). By authority, Jude references the power that rightfully belongs to God and is manifest to man through Jesus Christ our Lord (Matt 28:18; Dan 7:13*f*). The praise ascribed to God is eternal in nature because it is before all time and now and forever.

There is a word that is missing from the letter of Jude, but is illustrated by these last two verses: hope. Jude just left his readers hope who were standing fast in the Word. Let's take a moment and review just what Christian hope is. It is not worldly hope. By that I mean it is not the type of hope we express at Christmas time, or at work, or at raffles. If I bought raffle ticket #784 and the wheel is spinning and the drum is rolling, I might well turn to the person next to me and state that I hope I win the cupie doll. I might state to someone that I hope I get the Ford Mustang for Christmas that I told Santa about when I sat on his lap at the department store (I know, but guys will do *anything* for a 'stang!). Folks at work might stand around the water cooler and hope that they get a raise this year. Any wishes? Plenty. Any expectations? No, not really. Hope generated in the heart of the believer is an altogether different item.

Christian hope has the wishes and the wannas. With that we can be sure. I *want* to go to Heaven. You *want* to go to Heaven. But we are neither sitting on Santa's lap or in front of the raffle wheel while it spins. God *tells* us that we can expect Heaven and all it has to offer. His entire book we call the Bible is a blueprint for expectant hope. Is that not what the last two verses of Jude are telling us?

The letter from Jude began with a prayer in verse 2 for the brethren and ends in the same fashion. Jude closes his epistle with Amen, meaning, "Let it be so" which was, and is, the Holy Spirit's intent for the epistle.

Father, help us to ever be on the lookout for those who would tear down your church--the very family that you gave your life to create. Help us to recognize their actions and attitudes as being contrary to your will for your precious family. Help us most of all to recognize anything in our own lives which would fall under your condemnation. We don't want to witch hunt, but we never want to be found entertaining wolves in sheep's clothing.

Father, guard us in our time alone with you. Help us find the time to feed on your Word, and just as importantly help us to retain it, understand it and live it. Allow your Spirit to continue to guide us in our thoughts and prayers to you. Keep the evil one off of our backs as we seek for and spend that time alone with you. Open our hearts and our minds so that we may be filled with the knowledge of your will in all spiritual wisdom and understanding. Most of all, we want to walk with you in a manner worthy of you and to please you in all respects. Help us to bear fruit in every good work, increase in knowledge about you. Strengthen us with all power according to your glorious might.

We pray that we will allow ourselves to be leaned on by those who need to lean, to show mercy on those who are doubting and to help snatch from the fire those who are perilously close. To you, our Lord, be glory, majesty, dominion and authority, before all time and now and forever.

Amen.

About the Author

R F Pennington has interspersed careers, degrees and certification in oil and gas well drilling, law enforcement, clinical medicine and counseling. R F has held full time ministry positions for twelve years. He graduated from Sunset International Bible Institute and earned a Bachelors of Ministry from Theological University of America. For many years R F has focused on house church ministries and writing. R F and Dee make their empty nest in El Paso, Texas.

Published writings include this book *Allelon: One Another Understanding Body Life through the One Another Passages, A Healthy Thing Should Look Like This* and *The Bible Survival Manual: Mystifying to Manageable.*

All books may be obtained from online bookstores and www.bookcrafters.net.

CPSIA information can be obtained at www.ICGtesting.com
Printed in the USA
LVOW12s1125040914

402292LV00001B/4/P